Retirement: The First 365 Days

Personal observations, advice and opinions on retirement.

George Szlemp

ISBN: 9781697160819

ACKNOWLEDGMENTS

I am blessed to have written this journal with my wife Maureen as my advisor and editor. Her honesty, encouragement and willingness to provide many hours of her time and all of her many other talents have me wondering how I could have been so lucky. A special thank you to my friends Peter, Kevin, and Elizabeth for reading the manuscript and offering great suggestions. I would also like to thank Barb of Barbara Lee Art and Design for creating the wonderful cover design. Finally, I want to thank my children, Rachael, Cortney and Nicholas for encouraging their dear old dad's notion that he could actually write and publish this book.

CONTENTS

FORWARD

You made it. Congratulations!

Now what? Well someone gave you this book because you're retiring or you bought it yourself and are curious about what to expect in retirement. OK. Now what does that mean? I wrote this guide because I received a retirement card with the following quote:

> *"Do not go where the pathway leads. Go instead where there is no path and leave a trail."*
>
> Ralph Waldo Emerson

This quote may be good inspiration for someone who is twenty-something but I don't think so for someone over sixty. So, I've written what I hope is a useful guide for the whole first year. Please don't read ahead, if you can help it, because certain things should be experienced when the time is right.

INTRODUCTION

Here are my personal observations, advice and opinions on retirement. This book is a fun filled guide to help you appreciate and learn what to expect when you retire. I hope it becomes a gift-giving book to enhance this lifetime achievement.

I retired at the end of October and decided to journal my experiences every day of the first year. Sometimes what I wrote came easily. Sometimes I struggled with the topic of the day but resolved to just concentrate on what I thought and felt. Retirement is as different for each of us as each of us is different. Early on I became a student of retirement and read a lot of articles which addressed many issues. In the 365 entries you'll be reading I hope each one offers an insight to help you enjoy retirement. As I like to say, "Those who can, teach; those who cannot do research!"

Day 1 - It's Just the Beginning

You will need to consider two things every day from now on. First, this retirement thing may be your last hurrah! Second, only you can make you happy.

I suggest you have a plan and you create a routine. Set your alarm the same time each day and go to bed at a reasonable hour. Your energy will last longer and you'll accomplish much more each day.

Your plan should be very simple. Do two things that are useful and two that are beneficial. Washing your car and vacuuming the carpet should be done anyway, but now you have a lot of time in the day that you didn't have before. When you are done with your useful tasks, it's time to have fun – do something physical, spiritual, emotional or mental (cognitive).

Today I cleaned some windows and mowed the lawn, rode my bike and went to an evening meeting. Each action felt like an accomplishment. Life is good.

Day 2 - Trial and Error

It will take time and experience to really invest in your retirement. You can expect some nervousness and feelings of insecurity at first. This is good for you because it will motivate you to try different things and concentrate on the things you like to do most. Each day offers opportunities to do things that will benefit you and others.

I would suggest you split the week up into two separate events by treating the weekdays as weekdays and weekends as weekends. The best thing you can do for yourself is to create things to look forward to. I'm going to a concert tonight. I've planned and looked forward to it all week. This weekend, instead of chores, I'm going to enjoy community events with friends and family. These are just a couple of examples of what to do and not do in retirement.

How's that sound?

Day 3 - Sundays

How do you spend your Sundays? I think you should do as the good Lord intended. Take a day off and rest. Do nothing or do whatever you decide to do with an easy-go-easy-does-it attitude.

Slowing the pace and activity level is what most people are doing anyway. Everyone in the working world has been busy and needs a rest. If your retirement is going to be fulfilling every day, it's good to take a break on Sunday.

Some people go to bed early on Sunday nights and others stay up late. Moderation in retirement allows you to preserve yourself so you can drive as hard as you want throughout the week.

Can you do it?

Day 4 - Getting Started

Monday, Monday. It's the beginning of the weekly cycle. You don't need to start each new week doing the same thing. However, you might want to set the pace for the next five days of retirement and the creation of the new "you."

Sometimes, I read the Sunday paper on Monday morning. It gives me a lot of ideas about a lot of things. I also think it's a good day to review your finances and cost of living expenses. Sure, there are a lot of things to do that are free, but this weekend I went to three community events and spent money at each one. So be aware of what you're spending in retirement. If you don't know how much you spend and an entire week goes by without an answer, it's time to write it all down. You'll see why.

Day 5 - Top Priority

Do you have a calendar? If not, get one and start filling in events, activities and opportunities. Looking forward to something is very rewarding. The possibilities along with the choices you make mean you are being proactive. Organizing your time and new life will be a top priority for the next few months. As interests and activities become habit, you will become more comfortable.

I bet before you retired there were some things you wanted to do but put off until retirement. Make a list and put them on the calendar with a timeline. I wanted to paint the front of my house. Now the weather is great for painting so I'll get it done before the end of the month and check it off my to-do list. By putting things on the calendar, I get a lot more done. So will you.

Day 6 - Time to Make New Friends

I retired before my friends did. So, here it is almost one week and not a single one has called me. It's time to make new friends with retirees that like to do the things you enjoy doing. This can be anything from getting involved with an interest group, taking a cruise or just walking dogs together. It's bound to happen though; some old friends and some new friends will come and go in retirement.

I'd like to start a new hobby. I've gone a couple of times now to watch a group sail small RC sailboats on a lake. The boats can cost over $500 and the club is very competitive. Should I consider this opportunity for new friends? Pickleball, another competitive sport that will get me outdoors in the fresh air might be a better choice. Keep your mind open and when you have more than one option, try not to limit yourself. Let what you can physically and financially do be your guide.

Day 7 - Weeks Go by Fast

Wow! One week of retirement. How's it going? My first week went by fast and now I am wondering what to do in week two. Have you planned a lunch date with anyone yet? Think about reaching out to new or old acquaintances to start a conversation about what they are doing and find out what's new in their world.

Many times, in retirement you will need to make the first move. Step one is exploring your options. Step two is acting. I'm not particularly out going so I may have to put myself out there several times to get comfortable. A couple of nights ago, I went to a coffee meet-up after a formal gathering. I'm going again tonight to see how I feel the second time out. Everyone was friendly, welcoming me as a newcomer. Will they remember me and treat me the same way? Make the move and worry about it later. Better yet, don't worry at all!

Day 8 - Get a Recipe

Today is Friday. If I were working, I would be excited about the end of the work week and the beginning of the weekend. I would probably know what I was doing when I got home in the evening and could start to relax. Maybe I'd go out to dinner or stay home and call it pizza night. I hope the same is true now.

In retirement I think both Fridays and Mondays have a special place in your scheduling of activities, chores and want-to-do's. Your weekend starts when you decide. I'll be busy until around 4 PM. Then I'm going to start something new. I've decided that once a week I'll plan and cook a special meal. Tonight's selection is jambalaya. If you're not much of a cook, no worries. Neither am I. Just follow the recipe. It's going to be mmm-mmm good!

Day 9 - Don't be Shy

Make friends wherever you go. I've had many more conversations with strangers since I retired than I ever had before. Besides having the time to listen and learn, I'm not in a hurry and I'm not trying to prove anything to anyone. What freedom to be able to explore, even things I've never heard of before.

Today I learned about Moringa. I bet you've probably never heard of it and don't have a jeopardy's chance of guessing what it might be. I also spoke to a husband and wife, business owners, who experienced some of the best and worst things imaginable.

Later, I went to the beach and a total stranger came over and started talking about what he does and where he's been. Two episodes today of being friendly with new people made my day. Communicating to new people may be challenging, but you are building up your confidence and sharing what you have to share. More importantly, you're learning new things from others who are sharing what they know with you. I usually learn more when I listen than when I speak. Now that's something to talk about at the dinner table tonight.

Day 10 - It's Going to Rain

It was bound to happen – a very cold or rainy Sunday. You really don't want to go outside. This weather might even last for more than one day. When you were working, it may have been a disappointment, or a chance to take it easy. But you are retired now, so what are you thinking and what are your options?

First and foremost, I think your expectations in retirement need to change. Secondly, retired or not, everyone should have a Plan B. You're lucky, because whatever you decide to do, you can continue the next day or week. If you're disappointed about the weather and it's not allowing you to do what you planned, act fast and come up with a new plan. Since it's Sunday, I'm going to choose something that I wouldn't choose as a weekday activity. I think I'll go see a movie.

What are you going to do?

Day 11 - Identity Anxiety

Sunday night during my working days, I always regarded as a time to prepare for Monday. I didn't want to be too tired for work. For two days I didn't think about work and then Sunday night I'd start thinking about it again and all that comes with it.

I have to admit that, now that I am retired, I still get anxious on Sunday nights. But instead of being anxious about the work week, I now have anxiety over not having a job or a place to work.

If you're at all like me, your identity and the work you did may be one in the same. It doesn't matter how much you were paid for your services, if your identity was wrapped into whatever you did for a living, it may take some time before this anxiety subsides.

Be cautious about picking up the same career-driven habits in retirement. Playing more golf may not make you a champion, but sharing your experiences, strengths and hopes with new people and old friends just might help ease the anxiety and reveal who you really are. Fair?

Day 12 - Old Friends Give Good Advice

You are going to meet with people from your past who are also retired. You might consider comparing your retirement to theirs. Not a good idea. I had lunch with an old college friend who was visiting the area from out of town. We don't speak to each other often outside of these brief encounters. We share one common interest with great passion -- art. Beyond that, the only thing we have in common is that we are both retired.

My friend asked me if I had a plan in retirement. My simple answer was yes. My new job is to stay healthy. The rest, I plan to figure out later because retirement in these first two weeks has been a trial and error experience. My own advice is to let go of what you think you know and really listen to what others have to say.

I've reached out to friends who have been retired for more than five years. They all have plenty to say and offer good advice. So far, the best advice I've received is to keep doing what you like, discover new things and don't sweat the rest. Learn to relax.

Day 13 - Cashflow and Free Time: A Delicate Balancing Act

I got my final check from work and in about a week I will need to start modifying my spending. I won't receive my first social security payment for 60 days. Now what? I have a basic budget based on my previous needs. But I understand that most retired folks, including me, don't necessarily have as much money as they did before, nor do they typically spend as much as they did when they were working. I don't have a mortgage or any debt and I'm fortunate in this regard. My health is fine and I feel good. But, as you and I both know, everything could change tomorrow.

I have been surprised that time does seem to pass differently in retirement. I have slowed down the pace of the day-to-day and now have more time to do a better job with whatever I choose to do. I don't rush from one activity to the next. I will need to spend more time considering my cashflow and weighing my needs and wants.

It's not just about being able to afford to do something or buy something. Retirement has made me the boss of both my time and money. I want to make wise decisions and strike a good balance between how to spend my free time and how much money to spend. I've started to use a calendar and keep track of receipts. Every good boss does these things – plan, schedule and review.

Day 14 - Things Change, So Have I

Two weeks of retirement and I already have developed both good and bad habits. When I worked, I walked at least three miles a day, lifted many heavy items and stood on my feet all day. None of this activity has happened in the last two weeks. So, I think it's time for a long walk. I'm not going alone. I'll bring Scrappy, my dog, and we'll both benefit. I am also going to spend time on my walk to reflect on the last few days. The conversations I've had recently have made me realize that my background, and therefore outlook on life, is different from other retirees.

My retirement and your retirement are as unique as we are. I came back from a road trip today very confused and a little disappointed. I visited the same four spots I did a year ago. I expected the experience to be as exciting as it was the first time. But it wasn't. Then I realized it wasn't the places that had changed, it was me. This may happen to you, too. Examine your expectations and you will grow from your experiences in retirement.

Day 15 - When the Time is Right

Today, I need to start planning for next week. I'll be going out of state to visit family. It's my first appearance in retirement and there will be questions and comments. The first thing they will likely notice is that I've grown a beard. I hear that a lot of men do this when they retire.

As you can tell, my retirement is moving along without a big adventure, trip or master plan. My wife is still working for the next few months. We will probably do something grand in the near future as a reward for a job well done.

I feel fortunate and happy that we can retire at this age. There are many who need both the money and the structure of a job to be happy. My former boss at a big box store, told me as I was leaving that he was envious of my retirement. Although just a few years younger than me, he had no plans to retire at a specific age. I told him, and I'll share with you, that change is good when the time is right, but improvement is better.

Day 16 - Set it Down on Paper

It's nice to plan activities and not be restricted by deadlines or timeframes. Today, I will finish planning for our upcoming trip by creating a schedule. I'm going to do it the old-fashioned way by writing it down on paper. I'm looking forward to seeing how I handle both the freedom from home and my first trip as a retiree. I want to put everything I've learned the last couple of weeks to the test.

My desire is to set a good example. I want to be of service and also have fun. A lot of fun! I'm looking forward to reconnecting with relatives and friends. I also want to be sure to get to as many things on my schedule as possible – such as visiting at least one museum, hiking in the mountains and trying out some of the local food.

Day 17 - A Random Act of Kindness

Something happened today that has never happened to me in my sixty-plus years. On the flight to visit the relatives, I napped. When I woke up, the young lady next to me said, "Here, I got these cookies for you. While you were asleep the flight attendant brought them around."

I was so delighted and surprised I said, "Thank you. Your act of kindness will go a long way." She flushed, I think because of the expression on my face, or it could have been that I got a little too close to her.

But I was truly delighted and happy the rest of the day. I hope from now on I will try to perform random acts of kindness. Being retired gives you greater powers of observation. I'll never know what that young lady was thinking. At the baggage claim I nodded my head goodbye to her and thought--are retired folks just more sentimental?

Day 18 - Mindfulness

Today will be filled with car rides and canyon hikes. We will share both the adventure and complete the task of what we traveled so far for. I think the balance of telling each other stories, giving examples of our experiences and asking each other questions will be the order of the day. My hope is that everyone participates and feels they are part of the group. In order for this to happen we will all need to give way to the group consciousness rather than dwell on our individual needs and wants.

None of our hiking will be too arduous or straining. However, the group may scatter from time to time based on age or ability. I plan to engage in many one-on-one talks and share private observations without dominating the conversation. We all learn more from listening than talking. I will try to be myself and truly be mindful of where I am and who I am with.

Day 19 - The Past Has Passed

Boy do I have a lot of enthusiasm. The weeks' vacation is about to end. I probably didn't need to talk about my last job as often as I did. I think retirees forget that family and friends who aren't retired are preoccupied with their own lives. Although everyone is somewhat curious about what you are doing now, their children, jobs and home life take priority over your previous job experiences or the details of your newfound free time and adventuring.

I felt calm and peaceful, but still excited. I observed that vacationing with family is different now. The time when my wife and I were in charge has passed. Our grown children have taken over that role. The best encouragement I have to give is, try to bridge the gap, but don't offer too much advice.

Day 20 - Surprises

There are always going to be surprises. Some of these happen when you least expect it, so being prepared emotionally, physically and of course, financially for what may come, will help when it's needed. I had the great honor, today, of having my daughter's boyfriend ask for her hand in marriage. I was happy for the both of them and thought it was about time. Yes, I cried happy tears, composed myself, and acted like any father would.

"Oh my! A wedding to pay for." "How soon will I be a grandfather?" "Will I live long enough to enjoy all of this?" "What advice do I have to give them?" These were just a few of the thoughts running through my head.

When I was the same age as my daughter is now, my father passed away. He retired in April and died the following January. Although he didn't live long enough to enjoy his grandchildren, and never really gave me advice on marriage, he did give me advice on retirement. My dad told me not to think I know the future. He reminded me that retired people save money to live a life in retirement differently from the way they lived life while working. He also said, some men prefer not to retire because they think it means they have outlived their usefulness. Most men, including myself, no longer feel this way. They view retirement as an accomplishment and a reward. I don't know why I thought about the past, while having a conversation about the future. This, too was a surprise.

Day 21 - Focus on What's in Front of You?

With every new week I look back to see how I am doing. So far, I think things are going fairly well. Today might be a perfect day for a few chores and some exercise. But I think I'll ease back into my routine as last week wore me out. It's important for retired folks to focus on what's in front of them. For example, I no longer buy green bananas. Buying in bulk and stocking up on supplies is not necessary, nor can I afford to do this anymore.

At my age, health is my number one priority. I'm fortunate enough to live in a warm climate which gives me many outdoor options for exercise.

If I can maintain an outdoor lifestyle, stay healthy and be of service, retirement will be what it should be – a well-deserved reward. Although I haven't really added any new activities, I have been able to do more of the things I enjoy, like bicycling, swimming and gardening.

If someone were to ask me, "How's retirement?" I would tell them that I am still getting used to it, and one thing for sure, I do not miss working and I am never bored. So far so good.

Day 22 - If You're Happy, Show It

Since retiring three weeks ago, I've been able to go to a lot of places at different times of the day and days of the week. When I was working, I'd occasionally venture out to see what was going on. Experiencing this now on a daily basis has made me aware that a lot of people of retirement age still work. Sometimes I wonder if I could do their job and usually think, "I wouldn't want to."

It's not a good idea to compare yourself to others. For some reason, some retired folks like to mind other people's business and tell you what they think about everything and anything. It's easy to judge, but just because you have lived longer doesn't mean you know more. I try not to judge in my day-to-day experiences. But it's not always easy.

If you are enjoying retirement, you should show it in your actions and words. When I go to a store and encounter an employee of retirement age, I am always courteous, patient, and appreciative. Sometimes I tell a joke in the hopes of putting a smile on their face.

Day 23 - Where Did That Idea Come From?

I woke up with the urge to purge. First, I'll take the dog for a walk and water the garden, but then it's time to reorganize. I have papers, clothes and stuff in the garage that should be thrown out. Most retirees have accumulated a lot over the years and should ask themselves if they really need all of it. Some people like to categorize items into four piles – keep, trash, sell and donate. They also plan to get through it all at once. That's not me. I'll do a little each day. Because I am retired, I probably won't set a deadline, even though my wife and others may think it is a good idea. I don't have excuses now and the desire is strong. I suggest an hour or so a day. It's about progress, not perfection.

Along the way, it's important to decide how best to handle the items you decide to keep. It's time to establish new (and good) habits. Regarding clothes and other items, once you purge, be smart about what you decide to buy new. Remember your budget and recognize that buying used could be an excellent option.

Simplifying and decluttering have their rewards. Just do it!

Day 24 - Appreciate Each New Day

Every time I've started something new, I've looked to the future. I didn't know what the end result would be but I got through high school, college, establishing and running a business with excitement, anticipation and accomplishment. Many times I was told I was lucky and I had a lot to be proud of. I thought I worked hard but could have done better. I'm feeling this way because a recently retired person I know died of a sudden heart attack.

I have been saying for a while now that my job in retirement is to stay healthy. It is and shall remain always number one. This year, four people I know have died. All of them were men and none of them was old or in bad shape. Each of them has left behind a widow who is able to manage financially and may very well live another twenty-plus years. With these thoughts in mind, I hope to continue to try and be a better husband, father, and example to others. Let's go out and share the health, wealth and time we have been given.

Day 25 - If You Let Them, They Will Take It

There are people, places and things in retirement that will dominate your day, if you let them. Sometimes we allow ourselves to be overtaken because we want to do the right thing. Just remember that what might be the right thing for someone else, may not be the right thing for you. Keep your expectations reasonable, be open and flexible, and check your motives.

The last few days, none of my actions were selfish. I was being of service to others. I didn't have any expectations, reservations or agendas. I simply went with the flow and was there to provide what I could. When I reviewed the day, I realized things went well because of my flexibility and openness. These virtues have never come naturally for me. I can either change and make them part of my retirement thinking or I can hold onto my old behaviors. I need to think about what's right for me. And I'll continue to check my motives. Is this being selfish?

Day 26 - Pursuing Needs

I've been puzzled about the difference between being needy and being selfish. In my way of thinking, when a person says, "I have to eat," they are expressing a need. When they say, "I have to eat now," they are being selfish. My wife has said that I am both needy and selfish at times. I know this is something I should work on as I really don't want to be either one.

Now that I'm retired, I have more time to pursue old and new interests. I also have time to pursue new friendships, which is a good thing since I really don't have many. I recently met a group of guys who gathered two or three days a week to race small model sailboats. At first, I thought that maybe this was a group that I could be part of. Why not, I like new challenges, I like to sail, and I want to make new friends. But I quickly realized that they weren't interested in welcoming newcomers into the group and there was little comradery. Their only purpose was to win. This seemed very selfish to me. I guess you can't always get what you want. But maybe tomorrow I can find what I need.

Day 27 - Day to Day

It finally happened. I lost sight of what day it was. I woke up thinking about what was on the agenda for Monday. Then I said, "Oh wait! It's Sunday." This was a good thing because if it was really Monday, I wasn't able to remember what I had done on Sunday.

I usually don't like letting a day go by without purpose, unless it's Sunday. However, I do have a regular Sunday morning routine. I'll make a nice breakfast for my wife and we'll talk about the day ahead of us. I'll also read the Sunday paper. If I don't get to it, I'll read Sunday's paper on Monday, which happens sometimes.

I'm really glad to have my Sunday back. Although many retirees lose track of what day it is, I don't want to be one of them. I strongly believe in the weekends being different from the rest of the week. Maybe this is because, for over 30 years I worked most Saturdays. I really enjoy my weekends. I hope you will too.

Day 28 - Old Friends

The last few days I've been thinking about old acquaintances. What are they up to and are they going to retire soon? I began reaching out in email, Facebook, and even phoned a few I haven't seen for years. My wife was surprised and said women stay in better touch with their friends than men do. I guess that's true. My intentions were part curiosity and part feeling I missed out on many old friends' lives. Plus, I had the desire and time to do it.

In the past, my motive would have been to compare myself to others. But I try not to do that anymore. I wanted to share my views and experience to better prepare for what lies ahead. Two of the three men I got a hold of were glad I called and said they were years out from retirement. The third said he retired but went back to work part-time and wouldn't have it any other way. I am now curious about whether or not either I or they will call again soon. People's lives go on whether you participate in them or not. How your lives intermingle has a lot to do with your proximity to one another and how busy you are. I'll continue to reach out because I see the benefit and appreciate each day more than ever. Be the first to reach out, make the call, and extend an invitation to an old friend.

Day 29 - Cashflow

I had some unexpected expenses arise. My car and home needed some maintenance and repair, more than I had budgeted for or anticipated. This sort of thing has happened before but this was the first time in retirement. I think I handled it correctly, but I will have to make some serious adjustments to the budget.

I have accepted making a lot of changes so far. My retirement began with a somewhat "plan as I go" attitude. I wanted to ease into a routine, enjoying my new-found freedom. Living on a fixed income I now realize the importance of planning and budgeted for the expected. Looking back, I don't think I'd have started my retirement any differently, but I have had to make adjustments due to our cashflow.

For those of you who can afford a big trip, cruise, RV experience or any other adventure to celebrate your retirement, great! I continue to be reminded not to compare myself to others.

Day 30 - Time Flies

Time goes by faster the older I get. Thirty days and nights of not going to work, worrying about work and having everything revolve around work have flown by. I did like working, it's just time to do something new.

I really enjoyed being able to travel without having to rush home and go back to work. I hope to travel again soon, and will start to plan our next trip. This last month of the year with the holidays and my wife also retiring soon, will require defining our retirement together. I anticipate she will experience all the things I have and come to her own understanding of retirement. We have shared the same work ethic and have come to a mutual agreement that now is the time to retire.

How and what we will soon share does intrigue me. I know one thing she will insist on is to continue to live a simple life. She wants to eliminate more of what I call our prized possessions, personal treasures and other valuable things. I told her all in good time. I'm not in any hurry.

Day 31 – See What the Rest of the World is Doing

A new month, new opportunities, new decisions about who, what, where and why, are my focus today. I went to a couple of shows last month, enjoyed them and think it's important to see live performances every once in a while. Museums, concerts, plays, festivals all need our support. The experience is always entertaining, it gets you out of the house and allows you to see what the rest of the world is doing.

Some people rarely get out and watch television for hours each day and night. I like TV as much as the next person, and can only remember one summer when I was traveling that I didn't watch any TV for three months. I currently restrict TV time to a couple of hours a night.

I fortunately live in a community where I'd probably run out of money before I run out of options for entertainment. My December calendar doesn't have many entries yet. I'll have to do something about that right now. I just love getting out in retirement.

Day 32 - Life is Good

I woke up thinking things are pretty good right now. I have established a slow pace and look for new inspiration and opportunities. Today I thought I should show my gratitude for all the nice things that have happened since I retired, so I decided to take my family and some friends out to dinner. Afterward, we went to a comedy club. Great laughs and a lot of fun.

Not having to rush or worry about details is what I appreciated the most. I still think about my financial needs and obligations, but for now, they are not a concern. I will start to receive social security next month so my cashflow will improve in the new year.

Today I tried to show my appreciation for those close to me. I feel like a kid again, all this free time and much less stress. To be conscious of my life and how it relates to others is what I will continue to concentrate on. I encourage you to do the same in retirement.

Day 33 - Apprehension

What a difference a day makes. I'm feeling apprehensive. Maybe it's the weather. I don't have to prove anything to anyone. I'm educated and have many experiences. I started and ran a business, raised a family, traveled and had many life trials and tribulations. Now I'm retired, so why can't I just be content with that? Apparently, I'm still adjusting to the past and present thoughts that fill my mind.

As a distraction, I started reading a book about the previous U.S president's life. Now, thoughts about my own life have taken hold and may even affect my actions. Can a book do that?

I was given this book by my son and it sat on my desk for a week. I don't normally read books. I prefer reading the newspaper, magazines and exploring on the Internet. I've lived here in Florida for four years and haven't been to the library. I also have seen a book exchange near my home.

I love when one thing leads to another. I started the day feeling apprehensive about my retirement, then read about a president's life, then thought about my own life. I think I'll add book reading as a new source for information and inspiration in retirement. Wish me luck.

Day 34 - Don't Let Fear Get in Your Way

Anyone can sabotage anything, including retirement. I've had some misgivings about joining a hobby group of sailing enthusiasts. I've been to three of their outings and finally decided it's not for me. It was a nice group of people, but too competitive. I'm also considering a new sporting activity—pickleball. This group has a pre-established membership and has set times for play. I would have to sign up for an available time. I know it sounds like I am making excuses. I am, because of my lack of confidence and experience. I'm really not sure what skills are necessary or how I would fit in.

I did recently join a music group without any real concerns but it didn't take long to recognize that I was the least experienced. I am practicing a lot, on a regular basis and am determined to get better. One thing I've learned about myself is that I enjoy trying something new, giving it a chance, and then succeeding, even when I feel a little fearful before taking the first step. I think you have to get through this part before the fun starts. I don't want to sabotage my actions based on fearful thoughts. Fear can be overcome with experience. Finding a friend in the group can also help.

Day 35 - Staying Positive

Maybe, some retirees are apprehensive about doing new things because it's been a long time since they have tried. With some encouragement almost anything is a realistic option. I continue to have an open mind about what I'll try but there are still things I just won't do. For example, I will never jump out of an airplane.

I'm not quite ready to develop a bucket list. Although, if I did write one, I would feel compelled to put things and complete them in priority order. I hope I would recognize my limitations and try not to be naive. There was a time when I was a young man that I thought I wanted to taste every beer known to mankind. After a few months, it became apparent that it would be impossible.

Retirement is an ideal time to try new things, see new places and make new friends. Just because you never did these things before, doesn't mean you can't do them now. All it takes is a change in attitude. Stay positive. Don't worry about being the best. I'm not a very good dancer, but I still like to dance. Try something you think you will like. Show up, be enthusiastic and remember your intention.

Day 36 - Prepare Yourself to Help Others

Caring for others will happen in retirement. It could be a spouse, relative, neighbor or friend. You have the time so being of service is the right thing to do. Tomorrow I will be driver and attendant for my son who needs surgery. It's not a lot to ask and I'm happy to do it.

I often think about volunteering. I told myself to wait a few months before committing to any more activities. Next month my wife will retire which could put additional demands on my time. I also got a call this week from my daughter who announced she's engaged, which means there is a wedding to plan. I guess I'm not anxious or ready to volunteer yet. I would first like to continue experiencing my new-found freedom for as long as reasonable. Maybe six months to a year will give me all the time I need to enjoy and learn more about myself so that I will be better able to help others. In the meantime, tomorrow I have to drive my son to the hospital for surgery.

Day 37 - Keeping Busy

Having something to do and doing something is not the same thing. Each day of my retirement involves a choice. Today I spent the day in a medical center. It turns out that the center over-scheduled the doctor and experienced other unforeseen delays. As a result, what should have taken three hours ended up taking eight. My son who had surgery didn't complain and I was there to support him. All went well.

While there, I spent much of my time reading and watching TV. I can't remember the last time I held a book for so long. I originally thought I might finish it today, but soon realized that was not going to happen. I came prepared, but didn't need to because there were plenty of magazines, many of which dealt with health issues. One in particular discussed every imaginable illness. I learned that laser therapy has many applications. There is even a magnetic machine available for depression. Reading these magazines and seeing how many older people needed surgery, reminded me, once again, how very important health and taking care of yourself are, especially in retirement.

Day 38 - Each Day is Different

It must be "help other folks" week. Today I'll be driving my wife to the airport. She usually drives herself and leaves the car at the airport. But since I'm retired now, I insisted on driving her and picking her up a few days later. So far, making myself available hasn't interfered with any of my activities. I am flexible and can rearrange my time when necessary, without stress or resentment.

One thing I've noticed is that retirement has made me focus on the present much more effectively. Now when I drive anywhere, I always enjoy the ride. "Don't worry, be happy" plays in my head. I decide what's most important and what to do next. Rarely do I go out and just go to one place. I make multiple stops; some are necessary and others are to explore an interest or have some fun. I don't like to waste gas or put unnecessary miles on my car. My wife says I'm cheap but I prefer to call myself thrifty.

Day 39 - Schedules

Having to plan ahead because of other people's schedules is on my mind today. I got an invitation to play pool with some friends but have to wait three weeks because others in the group are working full-time and are busy until then. It's no big deal, but it's a long time for me to wait.

I've always said there's hospital time, computer time and now I've discovered there is retirement time. My activities and schedules are very flexible. There are no consequences for not showing up.

I was really excited to get this invitation, because I told my buddies to call when they had time to get together. I bet they will be anxious to know how I've been and what I've been doing in retirement. I wonder if they'll think I have changed. My idea is to play it down. I'll tell them what it's like not going to work every day or having a set schedule, and how I've learned to relax and enjoy each moment. Or instead, I might just steer the conversation toward what's new in their lives.

Day 40 - Time Alone

Solitude and quietude, what's the difference? Today I am all alone all day without a care in the world. I will probably do some chores and clean my car. After that, I'll go for a bike ride. I bet by eleven I will be back home.

I'm back home now. I was close, it's 12:30. After I finish this entry it will be time for lunch and some quietude and solitude. This is an example how my mind thinks during retirement. I am usually very talkative and rarely quiet. My mind constantly reflects on the path I have taken and wonders what others are doing and thinking at this very moment. It seems the more time I have, the longer it takes to do anything. But that's ok because I then have time to enjoy the end result.

I'm almost finished with a book about Barak Obama's early life experiences. It's been fun to read because it follows his life before he knew that he would someday become president of the United States. I wonder what he is doing now that he is no longer president? George Bush started painting portraits and published some books.

I painted pictures in my youth but the only painting I'm doing these days is painting my house. I do spend a lot of time in the garden and prefer to be outside. There is solitude in each one of these activities. I could probably use a little more quietude right now.

Day 41 - Time to Enjoy

Each weekend offers two different days, that at least for me even in retirement, are non-workdays. I live in Florida, which besides the weather, tourism and a lot of retirees, offers many choices. In all the time that I was working in retail, I did not have many Saturdays off. Now I look forward to spending weekends out in the community.

One of my favorite activities is to go to the farmers market. I also like to go sailing. I know a lot of folks do chores, run errands and do sports. Each weekend I tell myself to continue to treat and enjoy Saturday and Sunday as two unique and special days. Tonight, I'll be going to play some pool with my previous work friends. I'm already thinking that before I leave for the evening, I should thank them and make a suggestion for our next get-together. For me, there are three parts to fully enjoying a planned activity –making the plan, executing the plan and making the next plan. Consider penciling in the next plan before completing the current activity. It works for me!

Day 42 - Easy Going

The only real thing I had to do today was pick up my wife at the airport. I read the Sunday paper, took my time and covered it very thoroughly. Then I decided not to venture off too far because of my commitment. Well guess what happened? The flight was moved to the next day. I felt like I wasted a lot of time by being "on the ready" but not really doing anything. I know it was Sunday and a day of rest but I could a, would a, should a, had something in reserve as a short-term option. I've known and relearned that this can happen all too often in retirement.

I tend to often rely on others to determine my actions. When I enter a restaurant and the hostess takes me to the table and asks, "Is this ok?" I usually say sure, even when it's not. My wife has taught me it is best to let everyone know what you are thinking and act with everyone in mind. Trying to be easy going is not always easy.

Day 43 - Give it a Chance

Put yourself out there and see what happens. I was looking forward and planning on starting with a new group of pickleball players --men and women my age who enjoy sports, want some exercise and are encouraging to anyone who would like to join them. I just got back from a two-hour session and had the best time. Why hadn't I done this sooner? Perhaps at this age retirees are drawn to a sport that they can share with others and show kindness toward one another. I know that everyone at some point is a first-timer.

I was not surprised at the genuine welcome I received but I didn't realize how good it would make me feel. I was glad I was given enough encouragement to want to continue. I should extend the same courtesy in the future to someone who is a first-timer.

I wanted to play it cool and did try to make a good impression. But there was a lot to take in. There were sixteen players all with different skill levels. I thought I fit in and tried to be encouraging and show good sportsman-like behavior. I always wonder in situations like this what people are thinking. I was giving them all of my attention and they were waiting to see what kind of player I was going to be and how I would treat them. It's a two-way street.

Day 44 - Decisions

Making decisions in retirement should be easy. The one thing we have a lot of is time. How we spend it and who we spend it with are our main focus. I have taken on some new activities and my interests continue to grow. Some of these activities happen three days a week. I can participate only once a week and still feel it's worthwhile. There are others who make a bigger commitment and the results are far greater.

A lot of people play golf or tennis twice a week and don't concern themselves with the scores. I, on the other hand, always like to improve, learn more and continue the quest for greater success. I am even this way with growing tomatoes, which I've been doing for forty years.

I realize my physical and mental ability play a big role. Mine aren't getting any better. I make a strong effort to maintain my abilities but really have to push myself. Because of my age and experience I try to work smarter, not harder. Since I joined a dulcimer group not too long ago, I've only been practicing a few times a week for about a half-hour. Today I decided to start practicing more often and for longer periods each time. Tomorrow I might decide to focus on something else.

Day 45 - Are You Up for It?

What's the value of challenges and goal setting in retirement? I set out today to bike twenty miles in two hours. I was six minutes over. I've done the ride a number of times and only did it in two hours once. I know it can be done. A few times I turned back at mile sixteen, twelve and once at ten.

At age sixty-three, it was a challenge, but I'm happy to say that I almost met my goal for this particular ride and my progress is an incentive to stay healthy. Each time I have made the trip I have seen much faster riders. Will I get in shape enough to ride that fast? Only time will tell.

Just to spice things up, this afternoon I will also go for a swim. I'll spend twenty minutes in the pool and then read for an hour. We will see how I feel tomorrow. I thought of one more fun idea for today—making shrimp and grits for dinner. I've made shrimp before but I have never made grits. Off to the store. Another new thing to try in retirement. My next new goal is to become a better cook. Bon Appetit!

Day 46 - Favorites

Thursdays have always been my favorite day of the week. Ever since college, Thursdays were reserved for a boy's night out. It used to involve asking other people if they had any plans and telling them what I would like to do. For a lot of people this is what happens on a Friday or Saturday. My wife once said after several years of this behavior, "You never come home after work on Thursdays. Why is that?" Back then my boy's night out sometimes got me into trouble, but that's another story.

I spent a lot of Thursdays hanging out, talking and discussing what was going on in my life and in the world around me. Sometimes in one night I could help solve the world's problems. If people around me could just do things my way, I was sure the world would be a better place. It might have been the alcohol talking.

Today, in retirement, I don't believe this for a minute. I keep my side of the street clean. There are still many things that happen in the world that I don't understand, but I've concluded that I probably never will. Now I'm more interested in having many life experiences and sharing them with others. I have my favorites and that's what's important.

Day 47 - Don't Just Go Through the Motions

Encouragement at any age does make a difference. You won't change anybody including yourself overnight. By following advice and being honest with yourself and others, progress will happen. I want to experience a lot of things in retirement that I am not familiar with. YouTube has been a really great starting point for exploring new things. Progress in any endeavor takes perseverance.

My family has been encouraging without knowing the results. Others have encouraged me as well. I think they are just being polite. As with anything, you have to consider the source. Each of us in retirement has expectations and a need for comfort. Only when I go outside of my comfort zone, do I see real growth. I most definitely am self-motivated but that's only the first step toward achieving my goals. It also takes time and a lot of hard work. You have to do more than just go through the motions. Have you ever had someone shake your hand without looking you in the eye? Your retirement is not just about the handshake, it's also about looking yourself in the eye.

Day 48 - It Can Add Up to Something

Accomplishments in retirement do happen. I recently was asked again, how retirement was going? I replied, "I am keeping busy trying new things but I haven't accomplished much." The response to that was from a friend of mine who said, "My mother retired at sixty-two and for twenty years she hasn't done a thing, gone anywhere or ever complained about it." He said, "I always wonder why she doesn't seem to care."

I immediately thought of my grandmother who lived to the age of 105 and didn't do much for her last forty years. I can't ask either one of them about their retirement but I sure wish I could, now. Each of us can ask ourselves, "What have I accomplished?"

I must confess I read a lot of newspapers, and guess what I seem to read on many occasions? The obituary section usually gets my attention. Some obituaries list a lot of accomplishments, some don't. But whether there are a lot or just a few accomplishments, I wonder, was this person happy. What can I accomplish next? Will it make me happy?

Day 49 - The Holidays

Whether you have big plans or small plans, the holidays are here. I'm not sure why, but for some reason on this holiday, I am really missing those who have passed away.

People make a big deal about the December holidays. It's the one time of year people ask others, "What are you doing for the holiday?" When you go back to work, it's "How was your holiday?" But this is the first time since retiring that I won't be going back to work. So, I'm wondering, what will I do after the holidays. January was a slow time at work for me. Now things will be even slower. So slow, that I don't think I'll like it because I'm not used to it.

This year, one of my daughter's will be in England. The other one will be in Asia. My brother and his family will be in Costa Rica. They all made these plans some time ago. I am not really jealous they went anywhere. I just wish I could have gone with them. I guess during the holidays you should plan ahead and if not, enjoy the ones you are with. Sound familiar?

Day 50 - Reflections

I spent a lot of time thinking about the last year especially during the time between Christmas and New Year's. I am looking around at what still needs to be done and wondering why I haven't done them and what order should I do them in? We all need priorities.

Today I'll be cleaning up after dinner. I don't have decorations to deal with but I really saw some great displays in the neighborhood. Putting decorations on the outside of your home for all to enjoy seems like a very nice neighborly thing to do. The people that go all-out must love it. The rest of us decide to what extent we want to get involved? That seems to be the question we ask ourselves for almost everything.

My involvement with anything I choose to do has fewer restraints now that I'm retired. I can say, "Hey, I have time for that, that sounds good, I've never done that before." I will still have many questions about the details, but it really doesn't have to be complicated. With the new year, I hope to have more of a "Just do it and don't worry as much," attitude. Getting started has always been the hardest thing for me to do. Each time when I'm done, I say the same thing, "That wasn't so bad."

Day 51 - Hobbies and Interests

I have a lot of plants that need to be watered and cared for. Everyone who sees them says I have a lot of unusual plants and it must be a hobby or interest. I've always had too many plants. They make up a large part of my environment both inside and out. I like the variety and watching them grow, especially the flowers.

Every day I spend at least fifteen to thirty minutes observing them and providing for their needs. To anyone else it may seem like work but for me it's therapeutic. Mowing the lawn and washing the car are also things I actually like to do. They might not be as interesting but I look forward to the simple tasks and see the improvements as something both necessary and worthwhile.

In some respect, it may be maintenance. I could have someone else do it. If I were very busy or just plain hated it, I might see it differently. But I have been a hands-on guy most of my life. Now that I am retired, the enjoyment factor plays a bigger role. I try not to do things only because I don't have anything better to do. If you don't like something in retirement, don't do it.

Some people find pleasure in doing common tasks. Don't be so quick to judge them. Maybe I'll take it easy tomorrow and go fishing.

Day 52 - Do it Alone

I didn't go fishing today like I thought I would. I like to fish but usually would rather go with someone.

I remember a lot of fishing stories and they all involve others. I once went fishing with a friend younger than me. I told him he was very good, must have had a lot of practice and asked if he was taught by this dad. He said his dad never fished. In fact, he said he often asked him to go with him. His dad's response was, "When the grocery store runs out of fish, maybe then I'll go fishing."

I do a lot of things alone but generally believe it would be both different and more fun to go with others. I enjoy it because it provides an opportunity to encourage each other and share in the experience. I've done a lot of bike riding during my retirement. I go where and when and how fast I choose. I have also gone riding with one or more enthusiasts and it definitely is different. Whether it's fishing or bike riding, alone or with someone else, being in the present is what it's all about. It's important to live in the now. I think about this even when I am watering my plants.

Day 53 - Routines

There are short and long days and short and long nights. It all depends on how I spend my time. Some days I pack a lot in and other days I spread things out. I'm not quite sure if and when I will go with the flow, having nothing in mind for days on end.

As the days and nights pass, I seem to have a more relaxed approach to retirement. I wonder how I will feel after six months of this new lifestyle. I definitely have more energy and am less fatigued than I was when I was working, unless I don't eat well or get enough sleep. My dog walk today was quick and easy. Before retirement when I walked the dog, I would come home a little fatigued.

My typical routine now is to get out of bed at seven-thirty, keep busy until dinner and go to sleep by eleven. While it's about the same as when I was working, I enjoy more flexibility and variety with each day. Many retirees I've spoken with, also have a routine. I hope I can remain as willing, honest and open-minded as possible to fine-tune my routine as time goes on.

Day 54 - Improvements

Is there such a thing as self-improvement in retirement? I didn't always think that change was good and improvement was better. I recently worked at Lowe's Home Improvement store and their motto was never stop improving. They also added love where you live.

Maintaining my home does involve making some changes on a daily, weekly, monthly and yearly basis. I am starting to think I should apply the same idea to retirement. My life has changed in retirement but have I made or will I make any improvements?

The first improvements I started to make in retirement were landscaping around the house and organizing the home and garage, which I still have not been completed. I wonder why? It seems like old habits are hard to break. If you don't have to do something, why do it? The answer is simple. It will improve and change your life and living conditions. We may not always know why things don't get done. There are a lot of good excuses – competing priorities, lack of experience, desire or money. Sometimes all it takes is a short walk around the block or a book or magazine article to get inspired. Excuses don't go away in retirement, you just have fewer of them.

Day 55 - Death

When you reach retirement age, more people you know will die. I got some news last night that really bothered me. A very nice gentleman who was a neighbor in my previous town died unexpectedly. I, of course, had a lot of questions. This now totaled four men that I know that have died in the last year-and-a-half. Each time I thought about their spouses and how they would adjust. All of them were happy in their relationships and I thought of them as a couple. I know a loss like this is very difficult. Illness and death are not uncommon but it is through our families that we are able to get through it all. It is a sad truth for everyone, and we need to do our part to comfort others.

In my life my grandfather and father both died years before their spouses. Neither one remarried and did the best they could. Family was there for them. I rarely give thought to what I would do if my spouse died. I guess I'll think about it if it happens. This passing has given me a jolt and is another truth about what happens in retirement.

Day 56 - Time Passes

I am still saddened about my neighbor's death. This feeling may linger until my mind goes through it all and time passes. The one thing I noticed is how people, places and things continue to irritate me when I am not at peace. Give me a reason for being agitated and I will grab onto it even in grief. I have been familiar with the serenity prayer for almost sixteen years. It does work by reminding us to let go. We are not in charge. You may not like accepting people, places and things or having courage to ask for help. I learned long ago I like to stew, argue about the truth and show you a thing or two. I also have learned in this short period of retirement that it is not worth it. It is a luxury I am giving up.

I know I can keep my side of the street clean. But sometimes I do blow leaves onto my neighbor's lawn. Dissatisfaction, false righteousness, and indignation are all fancy words for "not happy." As you become more aware of your actions, be sure to check your intentions. They may surprise you. Even after the passage of time, you can still make amends.

Day 57 - Be a Winner

I hate to say it but there are winners and losers in retirement. I know it's not so black and white and most times it may not even be our fault. I'm not trying to be judgmental or mean-spirited.

A fulfilling retirement, like life, is the culmination of what we've done, what we are doing, and, most importantly, what we plan to do. It's our effort that makes it worthwhile. For example, would you like to be the best player on the worst team or the worst player on the best team. The best player on the worst team can choose to continue to strive to keep that status and help others improve, or can just exert a minimal effort and coast. The worst player on the best team can seize the opportunity to learn from others and improve. Or just sit back and not do much which is what others may expect. What kind of person are you in retirement?

I played several hours of pickleball today and am not a good player, at least not yet. There are many good players and I was given a lot of helpful comments from them. I especially enjoyed the fun spirit of the group. I'm a little sore because I like to play my best and recognize I need more experience and perhaps coaching to get to the next level.

Why? Sports have a common purpose. That purpose is what we all need to understand and decide if and how we fit in. I know it feels great to be a winner. Good luck with the game.

Day 58 - Prepare Yourself

It's another weekend with projects and meet-ups with family and friends. Am I ready for all the fun? Is it necessary for us to be prepared in retirement to be successful, content, and have a worthwhile time? I question whether or not you can ever really be prepared for the weekend, the week, your retirement or anything else.

It's my nature to ask these questions. For some folks, being prepared comes naturally with some effort but no stress. I was sore after pickleball yesterday. Did I overdo it or was I unprepared? Maybe next time some warm ups and stretching will help.

I bought some items for a landscaping project for this weekend but forgot a few things. I should have written them down. I spent more money than allotted the past two months. What happened to the budget? I guess I am only sort of prepared for all these things. This course of action is not much different from my previous lifestyle so why worry or change anything now?

If I go on a bike ride and forget to bring water, I'll probably be very sorry and the mistake can cause problems. Retirement is a good time to use what I learned in scouting -- be prepared!

Day 59 - End of the Year

It's New Year's Eve. Party time! End of the year. I don't drink and my father died on this day. Enough said. It's also resolution day, a time to reflect on the past year and all that was good, bad and ugly. Appointments, promises and resolutions are all about the same. They're commitments to someone for something. Never make them and you will never have to break them. That's the simple way out of making changes.

I have always made resolutions and even shared them at parties. I certainly don't remember them anymore, and can't honestly say whether or not they worked out. I am retired now so why not just relax. I don't really need an occasion to have a night out drinking and dancing. Or do I? I have had my share of memorable and not so memorable nights out. I also spent a lot of New Year's Eve's at home, which back then, was not my idea of a good time. One thing I've come to realize is that being able to celebrate in retirement is a good idea, and something to be grateful for, today and always. Enjoy! It's party time!

Day 60 - Getting Out

Wow! I'm not thrilled about last night nor does today offer much fun. Tomorrow however, we are going out of town for a few days. Captiva Island is about two and a half hours away by car. The excitement and anticipation are greatly appreciated. The drive and weather could be better. I'm thinking about what our experience will be like there. It took a little planning and scheduling but I need a good road trip every so often. Getting out of town and a change of scenery are therapeutic, for the body, mind and spirit.

Ever since I retired, I've wanted to go somewhere every few weeks. I have been on only one road trip so far and it was great. Why do I need another one so soon? It's only been a month ago. I don't really have a specific drive to get on the road, other than the fact that retirement allows for more time for me to engage in one of my favorite freedoms – travel. I guess I just like to explore the world around me.

The place, time, and experiences all come together to provide memories and opportunities to share. I know traveling isn't for everyone. But you can still touch, feel, hear, taste all the sweetness of life. For me, a Florida sunset is beautiful any time of year, even just seeing one out my window. But, watching many sunsets in different places with different people is even better.

Day 61 - What's Going On?

Are you in or out of the loop? That's the question of the day. A recent conversation with a friend began with, "What are you doing to keep busy in retirement?" I listed my interests and activities. He told me he started out the same way but after four years he decided he no longer wanted to know what day of the week it was. He now prefers to be out of the loop.

"When you get there, that's when you'll know you are retired," he added. I told him that's not me. I read newspapers from front to back. I like to be aware of what's new or what's going on in a lot of different fields. I could probably spend half of each day looking and learning. I still haven't made many commitments about what I should spend the other half of each day doing.

My friend spent most of his working life in corporate America. He went to a lot of meetings and looking back he said he had accomplished very little. He made money and had good jobs but they didn't amount to much. His life was really outside of work. Today he won't step foot in a meeting but with everything he does he still wants to accomplish something.

I guess each of us has a different awareness or perspective about everything. We choose our directions and actions each day. Not deciding is deciding. The so-called loop can be many things. Most retirees have a routine and participate in activities according to their zest for life and what they think is important. My loop and your loop are different. What's great is sometimes the loops intersect. That's when we can share our insights.

Day 62 - Day Dreaming

Living in the moment takes practice. I'm sitting looking out the window at the beach. I'm in a private home in a private setting on Captiva Island. I could never afford such a beautiful place so it's nice to know folks who can. The wind is blowing, it's cold for Florida, and it's damp. It's best to stay inside for now. I think I'll just continue to sip my coffee.

I am the only one in our group who is retired and my suggestion to go outside to feel the wind and cold didn't move anyone. I think I was just trying to say, "Hey, the retired guy wants to do an activity." But then, a relative in the group volunteered to join me on an adventure, exploring the area along the beach to see some of the fine homes. I thanked him because I thought it was nice of him to join me and that I probably would not have gone out by myself. We noticed there were other hardy souls doing the same thing once we got to the shoreline. It's a holiday week and we are on a vacation island.

I was asked about retirement. I said, "It's not just that you stop working and don't have a job. My job now is to stay healthy. I like to live in the moment and try to do so more and more. Each day passes and I experience it with an open mind. I still reflect on the past. I think about the saying, "the past is history, the future is a mystery so enjoy the present we call today." My relative asked me if we had any plans for lunch. So much for sharing about my retirement.

Day 63 - It's Nice Here

Some people know how to live. This multimillion-dollar, comfortable and peaceful home on Captiva Island will soon be going through some changes. This place is not a full-time residence or a retirement home. The owners have a plan to remodel and then rent the place. They would like to share their home with relatives and use it as a seasonal retreat for their family. I shouldn't look back and say, "Why didn't I do something like this?" But, for a brief moment, I did think, maybe I should have worked harder or longer or smarter so I could have a place like this.

I don't know if I'd like to worry about two homes. Retirement is the time to simplify your life. Traveling to many places rather than having to go from one home to another, sounds better to me. Thank goodness I can say I am not sad we have to leave and go back home, I'm glad we got the chance to come here.

Day 64 - Try It on For Size

It's going to be a very busy day. Why? Because I planned it that way. I told myself not to have any unreal expectations and since it involves others, I should stay flexible. Sounds simple but I generally hold high expectations and would rather do things I choose to do.

I just got back from yoga. It was hard, worthwhile and yes, I should try it again. In fact, on the way home I thought let's give this activity the same consideration I do others. It was suggested that yoga will benefit me tremendously. I agreed and went to one class as a trial. Now I realize I am just as guilty of my number one complaint of others, which is to show contempt prior to investigation. In the class there were no other retirees, mostly younger women. I didn't feel out of place because I went with my wife. No one seemed the least surprised to see an older gentleman. Even though I was the only male in this class, there are males of all ages in yoga classes.

I think yoga can fit right in with my retirement philosophy that staying healthy is my new job. Sure, I could play golf, start a woodworking project or just pass on the suggestion. It's up to me to try different things, stay open-minded and give everything a chance in retirement. Trust me on this one, I wasn't too bad at the mountain pose!

Day 65 - Getting it Done on Time

Boy oh Boy! I sure can come up with ideas, improvements and changes in my life. Keeping busy is easy. It's actually gotten a little out of hand for many reasons. Number one is not assessing the time needed to complete tasks. Number two is making excuses for why it takes longer then I thought it would. Lately it's been the weather. I also often need help so I have to schedule my time in accordance with someone else's availability.

I did get a calendar and began filling in the events and dates as reminders of the important and not so important things I'm doing. The number three point is to set a timeline and goal. I started a garage project but it's not done. I should be practicing the dulcimer more. But, I'm not. What happened to swimming three day a week? This is my life in retirement. I can either get it done or not get it done. In reality I am the only one who can make it happen.

Day 66 - The Tough Keep Going

I am not as young as I think I am. I woke up a little sore from physical activity. I played two hours of pickleball and soon after felt it down to the bones. Icing the muscles has made a huge difference in my recovery.

I noticed during play that two others were wearing knee braces, yet they played a better game than me. They must have a strong determination and desire to carry on. These are retired folks who don't want to stop doing what they like to do. It was an inspiration and warning to me. I am just beginning to assess my athletic abilities and have a ways to go. I started playing the same time another player did and he understands the game better than me, including all the rules and techniques. He also performs the way I would like to one day.

While I am not trying to compare myself to others, not a good thing to do in retirement, it's ok to keep your sights on how others are progressing. To continue playing, I need to be realistic about my abilities, progress slowly, and, when needed, remember the ice pack. Others have suggested that some pre-stretching and post stretching would be good. Don't ignore the knee brace as an option. I know I sound like a coach, but I'm really just repeating what I was told.

Day 67 - Spending

To spend or not to spend, that is the question. At pickleball the other day I learned there are some much nicer rackets than the one I chose. Do I need a better one at this point? Not really but when I was shopping for one maybe I shouldn't have been so cheap. Maybe a midrange performance racket would have made more sense.

I have really old windsurfing equipment and the thought of getting something new is an exciting prospect. What value do retirees put on the things they like to do? Is playing golf four days a week too much? Can you justify playing bridge every single day? Spending your time or your money is all about balance, moderation and having an honest understanding of your motives. Retirees sometimes say, "You know you can't take it with you," or "What are you waiting for?" Be truthful with yourself and the answer to how much to spend will come easily.

Day 68 - Accounting and Taxes

Guess what I got in the mail today? Forms for filing income taxes for the past year are sitting on my to-do table. I'm not worried about the past year. We have paid estimated taxes for years and don't like surprise bills or fines. I do wonder about the new year, though, as it will be my first full year of retirement.

Income and income tax most certainly affect everyone in retirement. Every time I listen to the radio, I hear commercials for tax planning, investing and how they will affect you in retirement. My mailbox has offers for each of these. I have been to two or three seminars and strongly advise everyone to go to as many as you can.

I thought I was informed when I retired in October. Do you know when I will get my first social security check? I was told the third week of January. You have to wait that long before you get your money. I had to rely on savings and may need to withdraw money from my retirement investments which are taxable. At one of the seminars I attended the speaker said "It's your money. What are you going to do with it?" If you don't know or don't decide, someone else, maybe Uncle Sam, will. During this time of year, retirement revolves around taxes, investments and cashflow. Do some accounting and it will lessen your concerns. There's a lot of professionals who can help make it easier.

Day 69 - Pace Yourself

Each week I get halfway through and decide it's time for reckoning. I start with reviewing everything I'm doing and then I move on to deciding when I need or want to get things done. The pace in retirement is totally up to me. How much or what and even why I do anything is either part of a plan or it's not.

There are things people expect you to do and you may be judged on your actions. I seem to have become more aware of everything including trivial matters. My closet is a mess, look at that desk, what about planting those two trees today? A "maybe later" attitude won't cut it. The closet, desk and tree planting are examples of the mind and body not being in agreement. My advice is to tackle each task as it comes up. Then it won't be on your mind and you'll be able to enjoy more fun and exciting things. Pace yourself.

Day 70 - Sharing the Pain

I don't want to go into every crazy aspect of my encounters but it just happens. Today a friend of a friend of a friend who is retired, not in the best of health, lonely and in pain, wants to end it all. The sad situation was relayed to me and I was asked what can you do? Can you make a difference?

When someone is in pain physically, emotionally or spiritually they are not happy and feel slighted in their retirement. The sharing you experience puts you on the spot and someone's jumping off point is now part of your consciousness. There are these bad experiences in retirement in which we are not prepared to deal with. I don't have a solution beyond just being there for them. This man's pain is also my pain.

Day 71 - Keep the Ball Rolling

Reading, learning, playing, and trying new things never seems dull or uninteresting to me. I love each day of retirement. I've met a lot of retirees who enjoy games and spend time going from one form of entertainment to another.

Retirement is like a playground and there are many rides to try out. Retirees like sports, cards, trivia, crosswords and much more. They do keep the mind and body more alert, bring people together and make the time shared more worthwhile.

Many retirees are very talented, smart, aggressive, competitive and aren't afraid to show it. I've played many different games and never achieved any ranking or status. I recently read the great actor Omar Sharif quit acting to pursue a professional career as a bridge player. I am amazed at the number of runners, bikers, tennis players, pickle ballers, dancers, musicians and kayakers that are in their sixties, seventies and eighties. Something sparked their interest and they were motivated. All these activities have the elements I appreciate and I think they are worthwhile pursuing.

Getting outside of yourself, getting inside of your mind, learning, sharing, having something to look forward to, offering enthusiasm and encouragement, and passing the time are all positive pursuits in retirement.

It's actually raining right now. What should I do? I haven't read yet today so maybe I'll find a book and learn something. You've got to keep the ball rolling.

Day 72 - What Do You Need?

Making do with less is an idea I continue to consider in retirement. I watched a movie about Gandhi who certainly was on a mission to live with less. You've heard the "less is more" expression but what does that mean?

It's always been hard for me to let go of the comforts in life but I don't have any problem getting rid of stuff I have accumulated. I am nowhere near eliminating all the excess, but I plan to. I once counted thirteen screwdrivers in my tool box. Years ago, when I moved my retired mother from her apartment to my home, she asked about all her stuff and what would become of it. I told her to bring anything she thought she needed. We had a lot of room. It was a difficult move for both of us. Because of her health she had to give up the lifestyle she was accustomed to along with many of her possessions. It made me realize, that this might be me one day.

She ended up not taking very much. Later she needed to go into a nursing home and then it was bare bones possessions. She said in a way it's ok because she had less to worry about. I'm on my own mission to not add any unnecessary things to my life. I know I'll probably backslide because everyone likes new things. I know my children don't care about my worldly goods. It's time to reevaluate what I really need.

Day 73 - You Need Insurance

Getting to the bottom of things starts with looking around and asking questions. My wife and I will both retire before turning sixty-five which means we need to find and continue to carry health insurance. It's not a simple task and costs a lot of money. It's a discussion which requires research. Agents and insurance professionals are not always straightforward. The options are many but the deals are few. Some retirees in this same situation may want to go back to work and continue receiving employer-sponsored healthcare coverage. Others might choose to work part-time to receive benefits. I've discussed this with my wife and although working until Medicare kicks in makes a whole lot of sense, we decided for the next eighteen months to pay for our healthcare. It's an extra expense that we can afford.

Whenever I get in a dilemma regarding age-appropriate actions, I always think about my Dad who passed away at age 66. Nine months of retirement just doesn't seem fair. He always seemed to say he would do this or that when he retired and put off doing a lot of the things he wanted to do until then. Another man I know who is seventy-one still works full time. When I told him about what happened to my Dad, he remarked that everyone is different, and he likes to keep busy. He has healthcare insurance and doesn't have plans to retire, and I shouldn't compare myself to him or my dad. Well I guess besides everyone needing healthcare, we will all probably continue to do what we think is right for each of us. I personally think my decision was right for me.

Day 74 - Find the Right Balance

Mixing it up until it's just right is often a recipe for success. I've tried to make retirement activity slowly become part of my new routine. Each day or each week I choose what to do based on my level of energy or enthusiasm. The only other factor to consider is the weather. I remain very flexible and surprise myself with my determination.

I am doing three physical activities and now realize more commitment and more time should be given to each one to obtain the results I'm interested in. Sometimes I wish I liked to play golf because it involves all the things I like to do – be outdoors, be with other people and enjoy nature.

My current limit is about three hours of physical activity a day. If it's more than that then I feel my age. Fatigue or injury are not options for me. I've noticed when I don't ride my bike for a while it definitely makes a difference. Using different parts of my body in a variety of activities offers different benefits. Some retirees don't have much experience with physical activity and others may do too much. It may take you a while to achieve the right balance. Mix up the activities and have something different to look forward to each day.

Day 75 - All in Good Time

Peace and quiet, prayer and meditation and learning to relax will help you enjoy your retirement. It sounds good, but being still and not having to do something all the time is not easy for me.

When I worked, I was constantly busy doing a lot of different things. Maybe the change to full retirement was too drastic for me. I could have worked part-time and transitioned into retirement, but I chose not to. I committed to not working for one full year to see how it goes. Time will tell. I want to experience as much as I can and all that retirement has to offer. Before I retired, I thought I would work a few hours or maybe a day or two each week. I've come to the conclusion I am working for myself now and I just don't get paid.

I've decided what's really important is to stay happy. A friend of mine told me he planned on remodeling his home when he retired and soon afterward became a handyman for hire. He loves being useful, busy and the money is appreciated. Sounds good to me and it's working out for him. But, do I want to be a handyman? Do I need to feel useful?

There is and should be time in retirement for many things. The order in which you do them is up to you. Once my wife retires things may or may not change. Right now, it's time for me to decide what I want to do today. I wonder what that will be?

Day 76 - Looking for the Answers

I don't always know where to find the answer. Maybe there isn't just one place to look. I think some serendipity in retirement is a good thing. I know we think we are in charge, but God may have a different plan. My greatest fears are injury, illness and death. Sounds morose but when you hang out with other retirees and older people you encounter all of these things to a greater extent than ever before. The latest bad news is often followed with the expletive, "What happened? When? How?"

Sometimes it's difficult to live life on its own terms. I am teaching myself how to do this as I go along. I keep reading about retirees, talking to them and reflecting in this journal on what I believe. I have told myself not to reread anything. I don't go back but rather reflect on each day and respond to what has happened or what I've learned.

Each week I seem to forget what I wrote before as each week brings with it another one of life's lessons. The more involved and active I become, the more it touches me and I am affected. I wonder how I will be able to reflect on an entire year of retirement. I guess I won't know until I've lived through it.

I haven't been at a loss for ideas or thoughts to write about yet. My goal is to have my body, mind and spirit work together so that I can share some tips and a little bit of common sense. I really don't have an expectation beyond that. There is no other agenda.

I know being married for more than forty years doesn't make me a marriage expert. I don't expect that after this year or even the next ten, that I will consider myself to be a retirement expert. I'm just trying to study retirement to share answers to the questions I think a lot of people have. I approach each day with open-mindedness, honesty and a willingness to share. Sounds simple right?

Day 77 - Is it Worth the Time?

One thing I like about retirement is I can do research, explore and discover so many things I didn't give much time to in the past. There's a lot of information you have to get through to learn what's most worthwhile. The computer offers quick access and you don't need many skills. Be aware of what I call "computer time," as it can take up more of your day than you anticipated.

I already have a two- or three-hour nightly television watching habit. Now I've added a daily dose of computer time which can go on for hours. Yikes! How did that happen? Sure, I learn a lot and apply it to my life or so I think. I've come to like it so much I'm posting photos and even did a YouTube video. Check out Gentleman George.

I don't think my situation is much different from other retirees. I know too much of anything is not a good thing. I've also noticed that the more time I spend on the computer the more things I want to buy. It's such an easy way to shop. It's time to establish limits and acknowledge what I often heard my Mother say, "Too much is too much."

Day 78 - Getting Comfortable

I wondered today if I'm comfortable in retirement? There has definitely been an adjustment period for me. After you get your ducks in a row and your financial situation settled, you may want to think about setting some goals in retirement. That's something different from asking yourself what you are going to do in retirement?

When I ran my business, I probably spent too much time on maintaining and not enough on goal-setting and strategic planning. I'm not good at setting goals because committing to things stresses me out.

A good financial advisor can guide you after a lot of questions are answered. I've discovered today that one of the most important questions to ask yourself before you retire is, "Are you ready emotionally?" Sounds strange but most of us do fear the unknown.

It only occurred to me recently that I may be able to ease the stress of my new retirement life with a plan or goal. I guess I'm still learning, adjusting, and asking questions, but I didn't think it would take so long to realize this.

I have spoken to many men more than women, and maybe it's different for us. I identified with my job but my wife says she doesn't. When asked if she thought she would be comfortable in retirement her response focused on the financials. I am wondering how her time in retirement will be different than mine. The time hasn't happened and I hear some reservations about when it will. The countdown has begun. So far, I've played retirement by ear because I feel relaxed and enjoy my comforts. I better give goals some more consideration.

Day 79 - Going Solo

I'm not used to going solo. I don't like it. I have learned though to increase my happiness factor it's best to not set too many expectations. I am having a fine morning not worrying about the afternoon while exploring my night time entertainment options. I would like to go to a music concert and no one seems to be the least bit interested, available or willing for all kinds of reasons. As the retired guy, I need to remember that others my age who are still working may not be all that excited to go out at night.

So, I guess I'll just have to go myself. It's probably the first time I've done that. I remember going to the movies by myself and it wasn't too strange. I go on solo bike rides, walks, windsurfing, shopping and a lot of other things. This reminds me of the line I once heard – "When I'm alone, I prefer to be by myself."

I've convinced myself that I will just go to the concert alone and keep my thoughts to myself. It may be easier not to go but why deny myself the experience because others aren't interested. I think the only real place I prefer to be alone is in an art museum. I'm a patient guy and never get too tired in other museums as well. The opposite of this would be watching a sunset. I'd want to share that experience.

I may need to improve my negotiating skills in retirement to convince others to join me next time. The concert was great!

Day 80 - Looking Back on Mistakes

Do I have to make any amends in retirement? I thought of this recently because I have spent a lot of time looking up old acquaintances, making phone calls, sending holiday greetings, e-mailing, and doing Facebook and Google searches. I got many initial responses but not many have continued to pursue the engagement. There are physical distances, working schedules and family time to consider. There often is also a large lapse of time in between our encounters.

People move on without you. I contacted one friend that I haven't seen for over forty years. I told him it might seem strange that I've reached out after this long, but that's what some newly retired people do. He agreed and said it was a nice surprise. He was glad that I thought enough about him to reach out and say hello.

I was never one to burn bridges but not staying in touch with old friends does bother me now. My reaching out was the first step but I didn't know where to go after that. Should we exchange emails and phone numbers? Should I invite them to give me a call if they are ever in Florida?

I truly hope opportunities to stay reconnected arise on both sides. I have a real need to explore these past relationships and try to understand what I can do to affect them in a positive way. I hope they reciprocate. That would make me happy.

Day 81 - Who's Watching Who

Is anyone watching out for you? I have spent a little more time alone in retirement than I anticipated. My recent trip to a country fair was alone and I thought I must be the only one amongst the thousands there, that was by myself.

The evening concert I saw was full of groups or couples as I got there early and watched the room fill up. I wasn't too lonely because none of my friends know the entertainer. I was going to watch the concert no matter what. I am glad I did. I almost posted a concert stage scene but I changed my mind because I was alone.

I may not do this again, partly because I really didn't try hard enough to convince anyone to join me. Making the first move towards engaging family or friends is not a strong point of mine. I think in retirement I will be more persistent and try harder. Right now, I'm aware of these ideas but actions speak louder than words.

My intake of fair food was excessive partly because no one was watching me. I don't think anyone at the fair cared if I ate one or five corndogs. I wondered how much I really ate? My family knew where I was and why I went there so the smart thing I thought was to bring home a fritter cake. I had some explaining to do because I didn't end up eating any of it. I was too full.

Day 82 - What's the Difference?

How is this weekend different from any other? It's not! My routine in retirement just turned into a routine. I think routines are a necessity for some people in and out of retirement.

Many people think that the day of the week shouldn't really matter when you are retired. But I like the weekends to be different from the weekdays and plan to continue the do's and don'ts on each of these periods of time. If I get disappointed with the results or plan of action my solution is to have a plan B. In retirement you should really also consider a plan C or plan D.

A truth I found out about myself is that I'm only flexible about certain things. I have more choices than ever before. Negotiating the options is not one of my strong points. Lowering my expectations is now a daily occurrence and I wished I practiced it over my life time. Now I am almost less inclined to give a hoot. There's always tomorrow. I'm going back to my calendar and instead of one entry on one particular day maybe I'll list some options. It's more work, but I'll remind myself about being flexible and I'll get this retirement thing under control.

If I expect these changes to take place, I have to stop making excuses. Sometimes the best way to learn is by doing. You can fake it until you make it. I've heard that expression more than once.

Day 83 - Mr. Fix-It

Retirement may not be the best time to fix everything yourself. I took pride in myself for doing as much as I could with my own efforts. I did set limits on the projects based on ability, time and money. Now everything has changed in retirement. The list of things I can or want to do has changed dramatically, too.

For example, I purchased new faucets recently that weren't easy to install without a special tool. I don't change my car engine oil but I will wash the car by hand rather than go to a car wash. I choose to live in a single-story home for a reason and painting the place is easy. I won't go on the roof. I won't try to fix the furnace. I won't waste time or jeopardize my health or well-being.

You get the picture. I am not sure what my wife thinks about all this and I am not going to ask her. I think her one point of contention is that things don't get fixed as soon as they should. Right now, our ice maker is broken. It's not going to fix itself and I don't know if I can fix it. It's worth some thought and maybe a YouTube view. Calling a repairman right away is the fastest and best solution unless you are me. I can make ice the old fashioned way with a tray. If my wife complains, I might just tell her to be part of the solution and not part of the problem. I wonder how well that will go over.

Day 84 - Continue to Be a Learner

Senior expos, seminars and lectures are out there. There are plenty of companies, agencies, institutions and opportunists who want your business. I would say go to any and all of them and learn about being retired.

Retirees have needs that are different from other socio-economic groups. A lot of them spend a lot of money. We as a group also like free stuff. It gets us out and participating in many offerings. When offered a prize or giveaway, some coffee or donuts, it's hard for a retiree to resist.

I heard we need to age with dignity. Sure, we may be healthy now but there's a lot that is going to happen as we age. Doctors, lawyers, health professionals, travel agencies, investment advisors, fitness and yoga gurus, assisted living options, entertainment venues, clubs, volunteerism and on and on will be options for you.

If you don't take the action necessary to suit your needs, someone else may. Be informed, continue to explore and share your experience with others. One of my favorite things is to learn about a place or activity through a recommendation from someone who has been there and knows what is important for retirees. The more you learn about the options that are available to you, the better off you'll be in retirement.

I read that ten thousand people retire each day. That was another reason I thought of writing this journal.

Day 85 - Never Say Never

Who would get up at 5:30 am to attend a grand opening of a local grocery store on a Saturday morning? Not me! But I did and convinced my wife to go with me. When we arrived there was a line, parking was sparse, and there were close to 600 people already there. We didn't get there until closer to 6:30 and I was somewhat upset at my wife for not seeing the significance of the event.

Everyone was standing in line in the dark predawn hour to get a first-hand look, try some free samples and maybe win one of several gift cards. The top prize was $1000. I later read that two people got in line at midnight. The details were in the newspaper with a photo. I think it was a lot of fun that I won't forget anytime soon.

I saw a variety of people, families, couples, groups and even some singles. The excitement and services were well planned with a lot of sale items and incentives. I did it for many of the same reasons anyone would. Participating in a community event is exciting for me. We shared a common, if not strange, bond of participating with others to see what all the fuss was about. I may not have done it without the prizes and free samples. Being part of the group never entered my mind until I got there. I most definitely will do it again.

Day 86 - Making Adjustments

There is an ebb and flow in retirement. I'm still in the early stages of making adjustments and I sometimes second guess myself. Sure, I have some routine activities in place, but the weather, my willingness and how I feel on any given day affect my decisions and how well I'm adjusting to retirement.

Time was so much more restricted during the working days. I did what I could, when I could with whomever I could. Now I have a wait-and-see attitude. What are my options and should I prioritize them? I prefer economy of motion in my life. When I go out to get something, I don't want to forget anything so I plan an order of stops. I think of it as dispensing time and money within limits. I'll keep busy running errands one day and then take it easy the next. I'm not the go, go, go, guy.

We'll soon be having guests for an entire month, three different groups. For them it's a getaway, warmer weather, and fun time. We've planned several activities but I'm sure we'll make adjustments along the way to suit everyone's needs. I'll maintain the role of the host and may need to remind myself it's not all about me.

Day 87 - What's Age Got to Do with It?

Is retirement ageless? In all the activities I participate in, all the places I go and each encounter with someone, age is something to consider. It's always been this way but now I'm the older retired guy who is acting a certain way.

I definitely leave an impression. I am quick to ask how old are you? I also say that's great for that age. I have only spoken with a few people who retired at an early age. They seem to be the happiest. I think it's because they have had the time to figure out their retirement. Those who have to wait longer or are working as long as they need to for financial reasons seem more agitated and not quite as happy.

I didn't have a set time for retirement. I could have worked longer for both the money and love of what I was doing. I still wonder if I'll get a part-time job. Besides "staying healthy" being my new job, I want to associate with like-minded folks. I am not interested in comparing myself with other retirees as much as I want to know what works for them.

Day 88 - Progress

It's taking longer than I thought it would to ease into the retirement way of life. For some reason, I want to feel like I'm making progress and improving in each new thing I try.

I now play the mountain dulcimer. I once played it for a short while forty years ago and recently decided to give it a serious attempt. I practice often and go to a group music jam once a week for two hours with fellow musicians of various levels of experience and skills. I also play pickleball twice a week for two hours each time. In each case, I think I'm improving very slowly. I also try to be realistic about my abilities and desires to improve.

Coaching or lessons are not out of the question. I have a purpose in mind, a good attitude so I've been told, and like to help others through encouragement. As I watch others participate it seems like just being involved is enough. Not for me.

Maybe I am more ego-driven and shouldn't even anticipate achieving some level of recognizable skill. Can I take things to the next level? Sure, if I give it more attention. But I like diversity more than perfection. I want to be a jack of many trades. I use the Lowe's Home Improvement Store motto in retirement, "Never stop improving." When I worked there, I suggested they say, "Change is good, improvement is better." I haven't heard back yet so I'll make it my own.

Day 89 - What it Takes to Retire

Money! More than you think. How much depends on how long you live. I recently looked at my spending habits. The amount of money I live on is the same as when I was working. I may even be spending more. I thought it would be less but I have given myself some leeway for the first few months.

There are hobbies, entertainment, improvements, clothes, repairs, dining and travel which were added specifically because of retirement. The main difference of course, is you have to consider living on a stricter budget. When my refrigerator needed repair, it made a serious dent in my finances. I really didn't have an emergency stash of cash and, at least this time, it didn't stop me from buying anything I normally would. This will have to stop. I've given thought to both the monthly and yearly budget. My checking account has a minimum which I keep. I know retirement folks have varying cashflows but mine is strict.

Those of you who don't need to budget may have fewer worries but probably should still keep some rough estimates on your spending limits. My wife and I made a budget with an inventory of specific spending, leaving nothing out. It will be adjusted from time to time but we both agree it must be done and we are still learning.

Day 90 - Who are You in Retirement?

I have given myself a new identity now that I live on a budget and don't work. I'm still selfish and self-serving but I'm working on that. I've started saying to myself and acting with an "I'm retired" attitude.

The reaction I receive from others in my day-to-day encounters is not too shocking because most people recognize my age and have experienced this attitude many times before. After all, I live in Florida and there are a lot of us retirees here.

When I reflect on the past I remember saying "I'm married," "I have three kids," "I own a business," etc. Now I've added a new identity – "I'm retired." What it means to who you are dealing with is the fun part. The teenagers next door who listen to rap while playing basketball always give me an acknowledgement when I'm playing my mountain dulcimer. I usually wonder what they are listening to but I'm sure they could care less about what I'm playing. I'm old George playing his dulcimer one day and fussing with his plants the next.

Things changed when they saw me load my windsurf board on my car. They may have been in shock after I told them it wasn't a paddleboard, it's a windsurfer. They brought their phones out and looked up windsurfing on YouTube. I like being a diverse guy in retirement who still has things to do, has made a lot of adjustments and continues to redefine himself. Yes, I'm retired and expect some different treatment. I know I'm not special but I won't complain if I'm treated with respect.

Day 91 - Adjustments

Retirement is all about making adjustments in spending habits, time allotments, activities and plans for the future. I'm not any sort of perfectionist but it's been three months of retirement and I'm feeling pretty much the same about everything. Can I draw any conclusions? Given my financial, physical, mental and emotional state in retirement, I think what's most important is to be honest, realistic and content.

How to stay true to this belief is an ongoing challenge. I hear a lot of comments from retires about these issues and wonder how they maintain their positive outlook in retirement. They don't seem to worry about the things that I do. I live more day to day and don't project too far into the future. I see a lot of retirees spending money, going places and living it up pretty well. They talk about trips they are planning to take a year from now or even farther into the future.

One friend of mine told me that's normal the first year. It will change after some experience. He also told me when you're older, retired and feeling young you can justify anything. I thought about getting a sports car soon after retiring. I had to ask myself why did I have this desire? For me it was reliving an experience I had when I was young. I owned an MGB sports car and had a blast until it was no longer practical. If you are making large purchases, starting new activities or planning far-off travel, consider why you are making these decisions. Retirement is about choices and the adjustments can come later.

Day 92 - The Perfect Retirement?

Progress is better than perfection. Retirement is a variable and why even think in terms of perfect? There well may be a perfect day, or successful week or month you'll never forget but when surprises happen things become more interesting.

I try to make a commitment and then evaluate my performance. When I had my business, I learned that change was constant. Sometimes I went with the flow and other times I was proactive. In retirement I mainly just go with the flow, see how I feel, and decide on what needs to change from there. Business and retirement are two different things but maybe a more proactive approach might be appropriate. The times I was more proactive did excite me. It brought me to where I needed to be. Getting there was an opportunity and challenge. I may not have traveled first class but I still traveled. I'll see today if I meet anyone who thinks they are living the perfect retirement.

Day 93 - Celebrating Retirement

When should you stop celebrating retirement? When I retired, folks said congratulations and some added a good luck in your future. I was grateful for these comments and wonder how I can maintain the celebratory feeling I once had. It lasted for about a month and then I started to take this first year of retirement more seriously.

I'm writing about my first year in retirement to share insights with others but I'll probably learn a thing or two in the process, right? I've started to think that not everything that happens in retirement is always desired. So, then what? I've heard it more than once that some retiree's health deteriorates shortly after retiring.

I'm trying to focus on the good aspects without ignoring these facts of life. I want to continue to celebrate my new lifestyle with all that is desirable, fun, and what I've decided is worthwhile. Having and maintaining a positive outlook and acting accordingly is contagious. You will be helping yourself and others.

But don't let this behavior lead to over indulgence. I'm not just talking about drugs or alcohol. My era of drugs, sex and rock and roll is long over but, on occasion, I still behave without concern for the future and the consequences of my actions. I guess it makes me feel young again. This is bound to happen from time to time, no matter what your age. Learn from it without being too hard on yourself. Don't worry, be happy and celebrate another day of living.

Day 94 - A Day at the Beach

I live near the Gulf of Mexico and enjoy the beach, yet this is the first time I've been here since I retired. I see a lot of vacationers and of course retirees. I wonder what kept me away? How often I go to the beach now is up to me? I'd rather sail or windsurf than sit at the beach but that's not an everyday option.

Maybe I need to make a list of things I could do, should do, won't do, don't know how to do, would like to do, and not forget the honey dos. If necessary, it could be an addendum on my calendar each month. You know, "out of sight, out of mind," is true. I know sometimes I avoid going into the garage because I'll see the mess I have to deal with. My problem of avoiding, ignoring or neglecting is not good especially in retirement. This could be the reason why I'm at the beach relaxing, letting my mind wander and putting things in perspective. The views are an added bonus. Maybe I'll walk along the shore.

Day 95 - Fondness for the Good Life

After a fun-filled morning I was invited to a brunch and spent most of the afternoon visiting, exchanging, sharing, and learning about my fellow pickleball players. The setting was a new home and I sat poolside after enjoying some excellent homemade food served by the nicest hostess I have ever experienced.

Everyone there spoke of what they did, where they went; restaurants, golf, travel etc., and how nice it was to be retired. No topic was left uncovered and enthusiasm never waned. I learned a lot of things about retirement and didn't have to ask too many questions. I soon started to feel a fondness for the good life. It was right here in front of me and I didn't always see or know it.

Each of us was unique with different abilities, needs and experiences, but we shared the retirement bond. Today, what was important was our current retirement status and what that entailed. I was drinking from a cup of life and loving each minute and wanted to sip as long as possible. The sharing of our educations, careers, child rearing and travel favorites led me to think that no one really knows what's next in retirement.

I wanted to tell them about this journal but I didn't feel it would add to the conversation. The discussion even went to the family and friends we had that didn't have much of a retirement. It just didn't amount to much or didn't last long. We were grateful for this opportunity and we showed it.

Day 96 - Strength and Weakness

I still continue to size up each and every thing I have and do. I'm not the competitive type, rarely jealous or envious and the comparisons I tend to make don't work very often. I do however see and do things with varying degrees of involvement. A rather young retiree told me that he exercises every single day. I eat and sleep every day and that's about it. I think what's important to one guy may not even register with another.

I'm trying to maintain an honest and sincere evaluation of all the things that I find important in retirement and enjoy reporting them to whoever will listen. I try to consider my spouse, family and friends in all my decisions. Sure, it's my retirement but no man is an island.

Retirement is not just a balance of actions, it's a call for action. I keep telling myself, it's your retirement, now make the best of it by trying different things. This can be even more revealing than concentrating on just a few. Dedication is a great virtue and I hope to evaluate my strengths based on many different options. I'll overcome my weakness when it makes me weak.

Day 97 - Leader of the Pack

People who are retired don't always act or think like they did before they retired. So many times in the last few weeks I've joined groups of retirees who have expressed a lot of enthusiasm, offered encouragement and were very willing to take on new responsibilities. Each group had an assigned leader who was initially not sure of what they were getting into and wanted to have an assistant or back up volunteer. That made things much easier and having a second in command was necessary as a training ground for when the assistant took over as the leader.

The leaders were as diverse as each group and usually very accommodating. In fact, I've never experienced such cooperation and willingness to serve. Each leader wanted to do a good job and began by leading by example. Majority rules was common except when the group members with the most experience didn't agree.

Maturity and retirement sometimes don't go hand-in- hand. I was surprised when some people spoke behind the leaders back and formed separate alliances. I generally believed you could say what you want once you reached retirement without having to worry about repercussions. Although this is true, it doesn't mean you will be effective. If you truly want to get involved in these sorts of activities in retirement and become successful, help the leader of the pack. It works!

Day 98 - What Do You Deserve?

I was never amused by the tee shirt that said, "I'm retired leave me alone." We may all have different views on our retirement but I bet there's a consensus on what retirees deserve.

One of the first things I noticed was the senior discount. Not only is it very common but it is often expected. We are on social security. Our money needs to last and being a senior is recognized in most cultures. I ask for deals and am not afraid to state my status.

The other aspect is questioning the possessions you have and need. I've started to ask if I deserve a new or better anything -- like a car, clothes, tools, toys, furnishings etc.? When you retire you are going to like to add some new things in your life so where do you begin? Once you get past the expense and deciding the affordability you may ask yourself is something good enough? What's the outcome if I don't replace or improve something?

I've seen this behavior in most people who have retired. I would even encourage them to treat themselves to new things because they deserve to live a little. Some of them seemed to act guilty about what they bought. A close friend of mine retired ten years before I did. I spent a lot of time observing him. I thought maybe when I retired, I'd understand his behavior. He lived in his home for more than thirty years and never made any real improvements. He made very few updates and fixed things when they broke. He never was interested in raising his level of comfort and didn't pursue new things and what they had to offer. He would tell me when I asked about getting something new, "I don't need anything else." He had the money and I would insist he deserves more. I believe in the never stop improving motto and think we all deserve to enjoy retirement with whatever we can afford.

Day 99 - Procrastination

One of the first things I did in retirement was to try and change my thinking. I told myself to not ever buy green bananas anymore. Before retiring, I thought about all the things I would do when I actually retired. I needed to learn about healthcare since my employer-sponsored program would end. What about other insurances, travel options, would I visit old friends and family, and shouldn't I create a will and do some estate planning?

After some thorough examination I determined that I needed a course of action and the time to do it. I talk a lot about these issues before I ever make a decision. Why? There's no deadline, hurry or anyone to approve other my spouse. The time has come to take action. I'm going to get down to business and deal with each issue with the calendar in front of me and a bank statement handy to address cash needs in relation to the budget.

I have become more frugal since retiring and have gotten better at recognizing over-spending and procrastination. Maybe I think if I don't make a decision then I won't allocate funds. Everything on my list will be done because they are necessary. Parting with money, feeling confident and taking action is what kept my business going so I have a lot of experience. I'll make mistakes and learn. The fewer the better!

Day 100 - Let's Have a Party

Today marks a milestone of retirement. One hundred days of free time has given me an appreciation for what I have rather than what I don't have. I don't need a reason to have a party and celebrate but, in this case, I decided I do. Why not? Throughout our lives we observe, recognize and distinguish ourselves with all kinds of accomplishments.

In my 12-step meetup group, people recognize you for what you don't do. I quit drinking sixteen years ago and never forget to observe another year gone by. I've often felt great all during that anniversary day and happy to share my situation.

My party may take some planning but that depends on how I define it. My carefree retirement seems like a party. Can I party and sponsor a party at the same time? On one of my retirement cards it said to "party hardy." Another said, "Live life and enjoy yourself, it's well deserved." In these three months or so I have realized that I haven't done either as much as I could. Who should I invite? Cheers!

Day 101 - Nuance

I'm like a child who when they discover new things acts surprised. In fact, I act surprised for everything, even things I expect. A recent visit to purchase a new mountain dulcimer brought me to an unusual place. I went to a mobile home park to find two folks in their eighties. The husband just happened to sell great quality dulcimers. I tried at least a dozen of them, each one looked and sounded different. This was not going to be easy. I asked about each instrument and then mixed in some questions of how and why he was here in Florida at this location.

He told me in this retirement community a lot of older folks like to play the dulcimer. This is true of the group I play with as well. I finally narrowed it down to two possibilities. They both spoke to me and I was affected by their nuanced differences. He reassured me that it was normal to feel this way. As a salesman he added, "if you like your instrument you will play it more often."

I was sold and out came the checkbook. While I was writing the check, I did have a slight moment of doubt because of two aspects I wasn't sure I could do without. Here was a possible regret. So, I asked myself if I could make do? I decided time will tell, it's much better than my old one and the sound was so great I bet I will play it more often. I also made a new acquaintance.

Day 102 - Fairies and Gnomes

I went to another party this week. That's two Fridays in a row and I can tell you I never did that before retirement. The hostess was single, retired, or at least not working currently, and just wanted to have some friends over to celebrate the progress of her backyard transformation into a fairy and gnome garden. At first, I didn't really understand what I was looking at and thought it was all a little strange. But the more I walked through her yard, the more I started to appreciate all the amazing details. Plus, I was charmed by her childlike enthusiasm for these playful creatures.

It transported each of us into her personal fun place to enjoy the real natural setting mixed in with some magical creatures. You could walk around discovering strange wonderful objects or sit and meditate with Buddha and Christ statues, gnomes, rock crystal grouping and many other intimate displays.

Everything was in multiple and people were pointing things out. I didn't think it was garish or overdone or even over the top and she told us it was a work in progress. She also said it was a reflection of a new interest that in some ways consumed her and the space. I really enjoyed the visit and was one of the last to leave. She welcomed us back and encouraged us to bring someone along with us next time we came over. Now I know a great place to see fairies and gnomes.

Day 103 - Anticipation

I'm not good at setting up an expectation without casting doubt and criticism. It's been a character defect of mine forever. And I never liked feeling this way. Any disappointment caused a resentment and I was not happy or fun to be around. It was childish and I'm an old guy now who's retired and I'm trying to be less selfish.

I've starting to change my attitude. I believe in a beginning, middle and end of each thing I do alone or with others. So, if things are not going as I like, there is always an opportunity to make adjustments.

When I anticipate going to the movies or out to dinner, traveling both near or far, and spending time and money to fulfill some need or desire, I want to look forward to each and every aspect that I can control. It's sometimes life according to me.

At the movies, for example, I like the previews. At dinner I look at the appetizers. Traveling by car or airplane offers so many options that I consider important. If it involves time and money I lean toward time. My fears are like anyone else's except being retired opens up the time discussion vs. money issues. To be relaxed, joyful, enthusiastic, playful, and able to live life on life's terms is a lesson for each of us to learn. My mom used to always say, "go easy" and "easy does it." Wise words, especially for retirees.

Day 104 - Day Trips

I took the family for a day trip to explore an island that must be worthwhile because one of our former presidents rents a home there. I wanted to enjoy some natural beauty and per my daughter's request I found this place and was very glad to share it. When you're retired you want to discover places that are not too far away, but interesting to experience.

I knew someone who told me they never left the Boston city area in their whole life. That's something I can't imagine. As I was familiarizing myself with the directions to the island, I noticed other stops we could make going and coming back and wondered why I hadn't made this trip sooner or more often. I think it's because I needed to do it with several people as an adventure for all of us. I plan on doing more of this with my wife on the weekends and other days when she retires.

My daughter's suggestion for a road trip not too far away has inspired me to plan another one soon with others who have similar interests such as kayaking. One idea leads to another. I could also visit a place once and then go back with others later on. Our trip today included many stops, a lot of time for conversation and the making of new memories. We only traveled an hour and a half each way but it seemed as if we were on vacation. I'm all in for more day trips.

Day 105 - Timing is Important

This week has been fun-filled with a lot of visitors who liked to do many different things. Today we are going to go sailing and we are excited to share the experience with some non-experienced sailors. When we got to the water's edge after setting up, I surprised everyone by saying it was too windy for safe sailing and maybe another day would work better. Everyone was disappointed so as a last-ditch effort I said maybe if we could wait an hour or so the wind might calm down because the late morning often brings slower winds.

There was a general agreement, so we waited. During this hour I worried that this postponement may lead to another disappointment. Luckily it didn't. We ended up having a great day sailing. My concern for safety came first. I'm the captain and therefore it is up to me to decide when the time is right. It's the same with my retirement.

Day 106 - Experience Breeds Confidence

I had the best time with my first time kayaking through some mangroves today. I read about this adventure but it didn't impress me until I saw some photos. My decision to go started after a new friend asked if I had ever done this before. They showed so much enthusiasm and were insistent this was not to be missed.

It was unique, challenging, and beautiful. We took our own great photos and I was impressed and proud to share this experience with some visitors. They wondered why I hadn't done this sooner. Even though I read about it, saw the photos and enjoyed all water sports it wasn't until I got encouraged from an outdoor enthusiast that I acted. I liked trying something new and seeing nature by way of kayaking. Although this was our first time, we learned a lot and have the confidence to do it again. Trying new things in retirement allows me to speak from experience. I can also say I've been there and done that.

Day 107 - Rest

I've been having so much fun lately that I need a rest. I have been going non-stop and may have to slow down the day's agenda. I think my age has caught up to me and I'll have to rest more each day. I'm not in bad shape but I think I just try to do too much in one day. Sometimes being idle in retirement is not all bad because it gives you more time to think.

I was thinking about mowing the lawn today, but that would be breaking my own rule of only doing work on weekdays and reserving weekends for fun and relaxation. I'm sleeping well and about the same amount of time as I did before I retired. I recently realized if you're about sixty years old you have spent about twenty years sleeping. What? It's true.

My wife likes to take naps and says they're good for you. My idea of rest is to read, take my time at everything and not worry about being a clock watcher. Sometimes I think I drive too slowly because I'm enjoying the ride so much. I know a lot of retirees like to get up early so they go to bed early. What's early or late differs from individual to individual and how much you get done is the biggest question. I spend a lot more time drinking coffee and reading the newspaper than I used to. I'm not a big shopper but it's more fun now that I don't have to rush and I don't mind if it takes longer. It boils down to how much energy you have, so make sure you get your rest.

Day 108 - Family Comes First

I've heard "family comes first" so often that I ask myself when didn't it come first? Our society has changed and many times in the past I was guilty of not recognizing this. Not anymore. I recently produced a YouTube video which I have thought about doing for a long time. It's both serious and silly but I think it is fun to watch. The only reason it finally happened was through the helpful guidance of family members. The same was true, when I thought about retiring.

I often verbalize my ideas and express my intentions. I wonder how often people believe me. It's usually your family that keeps you grounded and asks all the right questions. Everyone thought retirement was a good option for me. Their questions were the same questions I asked myself but they added something I was surprised to have to consider. They asked if I could picture myself retired? They check on me, observe and see how well I am really doing. I suppose there are unhappy people in retirement. I think there may be times when I need more help in retirement. The older anyone gets the more likely and evident it becomes.

I've learned sharing your retirement, both time and money, thoughts or wisdom, and using my experience as a guide, wins people over. I can only hope my family gets a kick from any or all that I do. I know it's still new for everyone around me. I actually look forward to sharing this time with the next generation that's coming along. I've been told grandchildren change your perspective. I can't wait!

Day 109 - Showtime!

We went to see *The Phantom of the Opera* today. It was exciting and beyond entertaining. It was a spectacle. I wonder how much entertainment is necessary for me or any retiree. Living in Florida is like living in a summer playground with natural and man-made fun all year. There are plenty of cultural activities and although you won't run out of options, you could run out of money. For instance, tickets to shows are expensive.

Some retirees become patrons or members and hold seasons tickets. They go to these events to both support the groups and have a fun time. I'm not sure if you can have too much entertainment but sometimes, I think it can become a blur. I've also learned in retirement routine is a good thing, but you should make sure it doesn't become dull. A simple alteration can keep life exciting.

I recently encountered a retiree who told me that he and his wife go to the movies every Thursday and see some good and some not so good films. I told him I'd only want to see the good ones. He and his wife share the love of movies, look forward to each week's offerings and like to experience a variety of life portrayals. Sometimes a good show of any variety will give you a different perspective and other times it may just be an expression of art. Have you been to an opera lately?

Day 110 - What's Your Role?

As this month has been filled with visitors each week I've taken on many different roles. I was the same character before retirement but now I can evolve into new roles. I'm trying to involve and even persuade others to partake in things and places they haven't yet experienced. I like to talk about what we are going to do on the way to doing it and talk about what it was like on the way home. This expands the experience and keeps everyone engaged.

I bet most of our guests who have visited lately, and I guess I'd be the same, expect to be entertained and given multiple options. Some visitors just take advantage of the open invitation but don't really want to spend much time seeing or doing new things. I suppose that's okay once in a while.

I'm trying to be the kind of host I'd like to have and not be forceful or insistent with plans. With different needs, desires and opinions I like to narrow down the options each day making sure that at least one is communal. I like to ensure that each guest is satisfied in body, mind and spirit.

Sometimes I'll be a field guide, narrator, driver, politician, teacher, problem solver, nurse, baby sitter, trainer, cook and most importantly, I like to inspire. I would never call myself an expert but I do like to be a jack of all trades. Now that I'm retired and have less stress in my life, I enjoy taking on these different roles.

Day 111 - Stick to the Plan

I always worry about the details in my scheduled activities. Why am I doing this now rather than that and what is the purpose? Am I just filling my time and deciding as I go along whether or not I'm doing what I want to do with who I want to do it?

I think it's doing fine and then I start asking questions. It must be my Curious George nature. I'm not disappointed in any decisions in retirement. I intend on sticking to the plan, making any necessary adjustments and not feeling guilty about being idle.

Sticking to a plan has merit because you need time to evaluate your choices. I'm flexible and haven't rushed any decision. I still consider my financial situation when choosing activities. I tell myself to forget some things because I don't have the money and it isn't in the plan? Having a plan or goal not only provides purpose, but leads to a more fulfilling retirement.

Day 112 - Bad News Travels Far

News from Iowa, where I lived for thirty years, comes every so often. Today, that news was about death and suicide. I wasn't looking for this news in the local paper. It found me because I spend each day looking at the computer for things of interest and updates from family and friends.

Today I learned of such sad news that I can't even begin to comprehend. A young man who I have known for twenty years, who has four children, a wife and more friends than I can count, ended his life. The outpouring of condolences, sympathy, shock, and love was beyond belief. Everyone asked why?

This one death has affected hundreds of concerned individuals with multiple connections. I had a restless night and could only conclude that if he only could see the love and sadness of his passing maybe his demons would have left him.

Both health and aging in retirement are natural occurrences. Suicide is one issue that does affect retires to a lesser extent. The fact that it happens to those of all ages shocks us into asking if there was anything I could have done? Are we the man or woman we appear to be? What are the signs? Life will go on and the sadness will diminish. Can we give it meaning? Finding peace and solace, sharing the grief, being more aware should be our focus. Rest in peace my friend.

Day 113 - Not Enough on Your Plate?

I woke up today with a big appetite but the fridge didn't have many options. I'm the one who fills the thing yet somehow other concerns became more important. It's not raining; I have the time and money so what's the big deal or inconvenience? I think I'm perturbed because what was important for today was ignored yesterday. Retirees may not be the most aware individuals. I forget more and more as I age. I hope I don't go overboard when I get to the grocery store. I often think, the more on my plate the better. I've been wrong a time or two!

Day 114 - Too Much on Your Plate?

I came up with another simple suggestion I'm going to follow. When we have guests and are showing them a good time, I will suggest only two activities and only two meals for the day. I might even apply this to myself. Our guests are usually on a vacation but I'm not. I do feel like retirement is a permanent vacation so the over indulgence happens more than I like. I've noticed many of our guests think more is better and fill their plates to overflowing.

It's ok. I don't say a thing. Retirees however, both the overachievers and underachievers, bring a different zeal to the table. It could be food or an activity based on all the options that are available. I appreciate enthusiasm but moderation is equally important.

Most of the groups I've recently been involved with have a dynamic with characters of every kind. In most cases they choose variety over quality. I once, who knows why, argued the difference between playing golf twice a week and swimming four days a week. I don't know too many retirees that do both and I question how well they would do them if they did.

I still need some motivation to participate and believe I'll succeed sooner if I surround myself with reasonable folks that are not too competitive or overzealous. I'm glad the retirees I'm around set examples and look out for each other. We are all in line at the buffet table of life. There's a lot to choose from and you can't have it all.

Day 115 - Staying Organized

My desk is a mess and it looks like a reflection of my state of mind. My routine is simple, manageable, seldom interrupted. But I've noticed it can become unorganized from time-to-time, I think partly due to laziness.

Neat is easier to deal with and I don't need an excuse for where I put the electric bill. Whenever I start asking "who cares if…" it sounds like an excuse is going to follow. I predict if you take this attitude it will lead to further neglect and more disorganization.

Retirees like me, with more time on my hands and fewer influences in the way, can become less focused. However, retirement can be the best time to organize your house and also your life from here on. Sounds like a serious undertaking but I'm up for the challenge. I think about all the time I spend worrying, looking, questioning, and even getting angry at myself. This is a waste of energy. Why not set some time each day to look around and ask how can I make this better? My wife has this skill and I admire her fortitude. Every so often I lose control and she'll save me from my frustrations. I didn't run my business like this, why do I do it at home?

Things are going to start changing around here…soon!

Day 116 - Follow the Leader

There are many group dynamics in the retirement community. Professional as well as casual groups have a leader or spokesperson who may or may not know what the heck is going on. Whenever I am driving a group of people to a specific location, I assume the role of leader and am responsible for the journey.

There are going to be back seat drivers, opposition, distractions and each individual can express a variety of opinions. How do you keep control and assume the leadership role? I learned in my many years as a salesperson that you must always control the sale if you want to be successful and close the deal. I try to keep things up front and give everyone all the details and address the "what ifs." I don't worry about all these details but others do, so be prepared.

I mention all the how, what, when and where as soon as possible. I hope the conversation turns to more interesting things on the ride to and from our destination. If you are a good communicator then you will be a good leader. Retired folks like to feel secure. If they know you are in charge they will go with the flow.

Day 117 - Count Your Blessings

It's not hard to let time pass without ever asking how's your retirement going? It has taken days, weeks and now many months to experience a variety of situations, options and activities to assess and answer this question. Asking a lot of questions is necessary when you are a student of retirement. You should also count your blessings.

I recently spoke with someone who is nearing retirement but will probably put it off for fear of a lack of money. He said he can't afford it. According to what I've read this is very common, even though ten thousand people now retire each day. I did almost get a sense that he felt sorry for himself and was waiting for me to offer some sympathy. We didn't get into how or why he was in this situation.

Another person who was part of our discussion was very well-off. He told us he worked hard since sixteen, yet he also felt he needed more time to accumulate the money for all the additional things he would like in retirement. It started to look like the haves and have-nots.

My gratitude attitude for what I have in retirement is just kicking in. It hasn't yet transformed into generosity. I am becoming compassionate, but I have set a boundary on how far I will go to help others. Maybe I should count my blessings more often.

Day 118 - Are You Excited Yet?

There is so much happening with my children and other family members. It's an exciting time for change. Marriages, graduations, babies, new homes purchased, moves, career advancements and a future life full of adventures contrasted with struggles, conflicts, and decisions which will affect many people in many more ways than they imagine.

Each time I hear the latest news I get excited for them and hope for the best. I don't know how excited they are that I'm retired. Their lives are being defined and they are gaining experience. They may or may not want to hear what I have to say. They are watching and ask questions about what I'm up to.

My excitement is in the enthusiasm I show. I also think enthusiasm is contagious. I would like all of them to be excited about something. The passion I have comes from within but that's just the beginning of my setting an example. I need to carry it out for some time to be convincing. I'm excited.

Day 119 - The Group Consciousness

Most of the things I do in retirement are with other people. It's more fun this way because you learn from each other. I'm happy to share all I know about everything, but some people aren't. We are motivated by others to participate and accomplish whatever our hearts desire. There was one group that I left because they were too competitive. I didn't see joy in their behavior. My conclusion was they acted this way to prove something to both the other members and themselves. Being the best or being better than someone didn't matter to me. At least I didn't waste too much time trying to prove anything.

I don't mind going at something alone to gain confidence and then search for the shared experience of a group. Whenever I get involved with a new group, I assess the group dynamics and how well I will fit in. Do I have anything to offer or would I be totally dependent on them to help me progress?

Each group has a purpose, stated or not, and it offers structure and guidance. Being on a team means being part of the team. Are you the worst player on the best team or the best player on the worst team? Most of us are in the middle. I don't mind being sized up. It's my retirement and I don't foresee hitting a home run or getting a standing ovation. I want to belong to a group which shares my consciousness.

Day 120 - It Can Happen

Sounds like common sense but whatever I do in retirement will only happen if I make myself aware of how it can happen. You can't rely just on serendipity in retirement. Slowing down, taking it easy, not pushing and lowering expectations are all part of the natural process of aging. This is not the same for everyone in retirement.

You'll hear about the old man or woman who probably shouldn't be driving who gets into a terrible auto accident. I read about this today and several people died tragically. Of course, this can happen to anyone but you have to be honest with yourself or at least have someone with you who can remind you of what's at stake.

I don't want to risk my well-being so I make decisions based on this principle. My physical, financial, and emotional state are typically conservative. I am very cautious when I go windsurfing and sailing. I have the discipline to be realistic and objective. That can change with age. I will continue to assess my abilities as I get older and tell myself "it could happen." Retirement is a good time to improve your awareness.

Day 121 - Out on a Limb

I never set out on life's journey to retire someday. It was not a goal or a dream. It didn't just happen either. More recently I started to give it a lot of thought. I didn't know what it would be like to not have a job or place to work. My many interests and hobbies managed to evolve and I had time for fun, travel and adventure.

I'm a very sensitive and reflective person who likes deep thought and draws conclusions based on options. I learned to adapt and was successful in business because of this. Now in retirement I have to rethink all of my preconceived notions.

There were plenty of times that I had contempt prior to investigation. People take risks even though they fear the unknown because the rewards that come with it are worth the effort. My day-to-day life decisions were made to fulfill my needs. I'm not particularly brave and have been accused of being needy.

My wife recently surprised me on a trip to the airport. The traffic was backed up and she decided to take the emergency lane. It was a big risk and we just made our flight because of her action. I know I'm not the type to do that. It was a decisive moment. The situation was nothing ventured nothing gained.

Retirement doesn't stop us from doing anything. It may seem like going out on a limb but I made the right decision and won't look back. In fact, I think I'll be braver and less needy if I'm given the chance.

Day 122 - Do the Research

I've had a week full of adventures into some unfamiliar places and part of me didn't mind not knowing too much beforehand. Our visitors this month required a lot of entertaining, both day and night. Most of the time they relied on me to lead the way and many times I was told I could have done more research. I don't think I disappointed anyone including myself but I've learned the more you know the better it will go.

When we moved to Florida from Iowa we didn't stop working. Our plan was to work for a while and then retire. We had been to several other places in Texas, California and Arizona before making our decision to move to Florida. We did a lot of research. Being informed through research didn't take away from the excitement of discovery. A greater awareness allows you and those around you to be more confident to fulfill both your needs and wants. You may not become an expert given the time you have, but familiarity and preparedness provide peace of mind. Retirees like that more than imaginable.

Day 123 - You May Be Taken Advantage Of

I had some service work done today and felt like I paid above and beyond what I expected. Many times, you hear about retirees who fall prey to suspect service providers, contractors, doctors, lawyers, insurance agents and just about anyone you put your trust and hard-earned money into.

The way to avoid this situation isn't simple as each of us has specific needs and wants. Being cautious and alert is the first step. If you are nervous there's probably a good reason so ask for help from others. Retirees sometimes don't like to bother others but, in this case, it is better to be safe than sorry.

Becoming a victim because of your mental and emotional state happens because retirees often become more isolated. Getting the word out about needing some recommendations will help. I try to treat everyone with the same respect and wait to see the response.

If you appear vulnerable, people will sense your weakness. Don't be ashamed. I am a six-foot man and during my store-keeper days I was robbed by teenagers who thought I wasn't a threat. It took a lot of trial and error attempts to change that impression. You've been warned now, so be prepared.

Day 124 - It's Sometimes a Lost Cause

I had to replace a lot of things this week. Each item lasted as long as it was made to last, but not to my satisfaction. I don't think the world will change just because I am not satisfied. I can however decide on who I'll do business with and what actions I will take.

A new realization in retirement has been to accept who I am and what I can and cannot do. I can't worry about all the details and rely solely on others advice. I can hope my tires last a little longer or I can read some reviews before I go tire shopping. I'm learning to accept life on life's terms. I like being optimistic and need encouragement to be more proactive. You'll let go of things more easily if you think it's a lost cause.

Day 125 - Who Knows What I Know?

The simple realization that we only know what we know was revealed today by someone I recently met. He spoke about how he appreciated spending time vs. money on the activities in which retirees like to partake. He said he has been retired for twenty years and has done just about everything a retiree can do.

Being kind and thoughtful were the first things he had to learn about in retirement. I smiled at the comment and thought how true it has been in my own experience that most retires are nice. When I think back on what I saw and thought of older adults it wasn't something I looked forward to or envisioned for myself in any particular way. Now I've begun to wonder and question how others see me in retirement? Can I share what I know and will it be beneficial to anyone?

Well I'm willing to share all my experiences and I'm sure most people will soon see what I know and don't know. You don't learn much by talking. When you listen, you learn. I was happy I spent time with this stranger. The last thing he told me was he won't be sad when life's over but glad that it lasted so long, especially his years in retirement. That's when I told him the first thing I learned in retirement was to stay healthy. He laughed, while he shook my hand goodbye.

Day 126 - Rent It

I have come across some retirees who have bought or are considering buying an RV, car, motorcycle, boat and other major things that they plan to enjoy in retirement. Many of them want to have recreational items available for traveling, sight-seeing and exploring the country. Each of these items requires some experience and knowledge.

I would recommend renting, leasing or trying them out first. A lot of these guys seem to get involved with more than they can handle in regards to time and money. People feel younger when they retire and the outdoors comes calling.

I know someone who has two boats. He'd probably sell you either one just so he could get another. This other guy I know has three cars, drives two of them and the other he looks at in the garage. He tells everyone it's a collector's car and it will go up in value.

My neighbor has an RV. I watch him set it up, clean and prepare or repair it before and after every use. He does all the work himself and his family and invited friends get to enjoy it. I wonder when I will get invited to share some of these boy toys? Maybe I'll just go and rent one for myself.

Day 127 - Break Time Again!

Somehow, I have decided that taking a break doesn't have to always happen after you've done something. I now take a break whenever I want to. Sometimes I'll take a nap because I got up too early. Other times I'll rest before going out for some late-night fun. Either way I think being older and retired means you could run out of energy. I don't want that.

Coffee and energy drinks work sometimes but in the long run they are not the best solution. I go to sleep at about the same time each night and set the alarm to wake up at the same time each morning. I have some regular chores in the garden and landscaping which gets done almost each day. It takes energy and it's often hot in Florida.

The endless summer here can take a toll on the elderly. I even take breaks before and after mowing the lawn. Late afternoon and before dinner each day I start to wind down with thoughts of what's for dinner and did I finish reading the newspaper? I now have a chair in front of my house just to be able to have a seat. It feels like retirement.

Day 128 - The Long Haul

I'm in this retirement for the duration I've been given on this earth. I can't say how long but since I hope to live a more simple and stress-free life, stay healthy, keep busy and continue to occupy my mind with things that interest me, I'll count each year as a blessing. I have no reason to hurry anymore.

I have a sort of bucket list with things I'd like to do that would be better done sooner than later. Whenever I think about all the men I know that have passed so far and how they didn't have much warning, I'm reminded of trying to live each day with more meaning. I do enjoy each moment and each day and night of retirement more because of this.

My serenity is important and I try not to sweat the small stuff. I agree with the notion that life is a journey and not a destination. I think I'd like to travel and maybe go on a cruise. A long trip might be just the thing I need. I'd also be happy with two short ones.

Day 129 - Staying Motivated

I have slipped lately on my projects. I don't want to start any new ones and not all the ones started are finished. I believe the front of the house will eventually get painted. Without a deadline, the weather is about my only excuse. I think lists are important and I've made some calendar notes to plan, execute and evaluate my progress. I've also ignored some day-to-day eyesores that could be crossed off and erased from the list.

It's time to take control and ask who is really in charge? You start with a need to add to a list which will get the ball rolling. Before you know it, you say that wasn't so bad. You stay motivated by making progress. I suggest that the list not be too long. Follow a schedule and complete projects within a stated time frame.

In retirement the problem arises because everything is negotiable. Who are you negotiating with? I must have an imaginary friend who I allow to live in my head. He lives there rent free and I still can't afford him because I'm retired living on Social Security.

I know a journey begins with the first step but when you schedule all the steps, it can become overwhelming. Take a deep breath and relax, you can and will find a way to do it. Where did I put the paint for the front of the house?

Day 130 – Insurance

Looks like I have to make some decisions about insurance -- home, car, life, boat, health and who knows what else? This can be expensive and only recently did I add it all up to see how much it would be. Lowering expenses in retirement is now a top priority. Adjustments will have to be considered. All these liabilities have consequences most of us can't afford to ignore. It's my first evaluation in retirement and if I can get it under control, I may not have to do it again until maybe next year. Once a year should do.

I consider these fixed costs since they don't go down from year to year. I'll start with some price shopping and ask others what they do. There are organizations to join which offer some group savings. I will look at all I can find. Many insurances have a higher deductible to save you money but I prefer a lower deductible in retirement? All these questions are part of the evaluation process and it's better to play it safe and be smart. When it rains it pours. But I have insurance for that, right?

Day 131 - Mix It Up

I have put a lot of effort into maintaining my routine. I'm strict because it gives me purpose and it's easier to put one foot in front of the next. When I explain my plan to others, sometimes I'm told to try and mix it up. Immediately I respond with a "No, I don't think so."

Why change something that works? The simple answer is because you don't know until you try something new. The convincing statement is "You only know what you know." Seems like in my retirement I've learned more about what I don't know.

I think I've spent more time thinking about making changes to my routine than putting them into action. When I get some information, opinion or suggestion, I consider the source. Next, I question the person's credibility and motivation. Finally, I ask what do I have to lose? Retirement was a big step for me and I'll have to be more open-minded about mixing things up.

Day 132 - Turn It Up or Down a Notch

Retiring at 63, living in a warm climate here in Florida and seeing the many activities for adults my age and older have kept me busy making choices. Retirement can give you a boost of energy and if you do it right, keep you youthful in spirit. You have to consider time, money, ability, need, desire and outlook to make all the right decisions. Based on what you like and the results achieved, you will have plenty of opportunities to turn things up and down a notch.

I find answers in the small details of each experience. Each day I'm given an opportunity to perform tasks at different levels. My youthful side says let's turn it up a notch. If I want something to last longer and look at my past history of experiences, I may turn it down a notch. In either case the worst thing is you can get burned out by losing interest and letting the desire slip away.

My mother got overwhelmed very easily and would want to give up sooner than I thought she should. She once complained that every time she turned around something was costing her money. I told her not to turn around. My point is simply that there are consequences to both action and non-action.

Day 133 - Even Keel

I am really into maintaining myself in retirement. I've got the desire and motivation. I've seen results come slowly and I can lower my expectations to accommodate my physical, emotional, mental and financial situation. At my age, I do see the limitations and accept them. If you want your retirement to be smooth sailing, do what I do when I sail my Hobie – keep an even keel.

There have been some choppy times that were not fun. I have put myself in harm's way and took the risk for the thrill of the ride. I've also learned that by keeping balanced, I can move along easier and safer. Shifting winds or bumps in the road can't always be avoided. Hoist the sail and even the keel for smooth sailing in retirement. It all works because you know what to do.

Day 134 - Keeping Up with the Joneses

The area in which we live has a lot of well-to-do families. There are many retirees but it's more of a family-oriented community. Between what I see and what I hear it's more important to me to identify with those who are retired. The families on each side of me have nicer homes and their garages are full of stuff. The greatest satisfaction for me is that my home is paid for and I'm more interested in eliminating stuff than acquiring new things.

My simplified life allows me to observe, rather than partake in, all the activities associated with raising a family. I have a "been there, done that" attitude about it. My wife and I went shopping today and noticed that every type of item comes in good, better and best which you can buy at a low, medium or high price. I always go for value but appreciate being able to make an upgrade. I guess I'd rather spend money on travel both near and far. There are retirees who can afford to do both. I hope they appreciate their good fortune. I'm not going to try and keep up with the Joneses.

Day 135 - Explain Yourself

I had to answer a lot of "who, what and why" questions today. This happens almost every time I meet new people in any social situation. I've been asked the same questions so often that I decide how much time I have to answer the questions and I've memorized some of my answers. I don't mind it at all because I can ask them questions and learn about their situations and how they came about.

I show enthusiasm about where I came from and where I am now. I should probably shorten my answers and wait for the next opportunity to give them the detailed version.

I think people form a more accurate impression when you provide more details in response to their questions. I'm from Iowa and I make sure I tell everyone how much we appreciated the Midwest lifestyle and how much we benefited from it. We left for better weather but I have fond memories of all that the four seasons have to offer.

I spoke with a couple from Delaware today and had to admit I knew nothing about that part of the country. They had never been to Iowa so we were eager to learn about each other's experiences. This type of encounter with retirees will probably go on no matter how long we live here. I better get my story straight because you can only make one first impression.

Day 136 - Get Comfortable, Then Fine Tune Your Retirement

My wife and I decided to look at each room of our home to reassess its purpose. What goes or what stays? What do we like and what works best? It's not a simple task so we started with the closets and storage areas. A little is done each day. I'm trying to do the same with my schedule and decide on my priorities.

Today I decided it's time for another twenty-mile bike ride to get more exercise. This small decision took both mental and physical preparedness. This evening I have a meeting that I attend weekly and always look forward to seeing the familiar faces and hearing some interesting topics open for discussion. Neither of these tasks take much thought, but do I want to try something else for some other purpose? I think I've chosen them to serve both the short and long term benefit I seek in retirement. I want to achieve progress, not perfection.

My goal in biking is to ride the twenty miles in under two hours. It's only going to happen with some hard work. Those closets are looking better but I'm avoiding my garage, which is a lot bigger. When I think about my role in my weekly meeting I soon wonder if I should expand it. These are random thoughts I have with most of things I choose to do or not do.

Fine tuning sometimes means having a tuner. I bought one for my musical instruments and now it's easier to play and the results are as great as they should be. Retirement doesn't have to have any sour notes because we can fine tune it each and every day. You are the tuner!

Day 137 - How Did This Happen?

There are so many things in life and retirement you just cannot control. I've reached an age at which I'm more aware of this as well as the various changes that have occurred. I have experienced many physical, mental and emotional changes in retirement and will need to continually adjust.

Technology is one of the things that I find very daunting. Today I tried to set up an eBay account to sell some things online. Don't laugh, but for some reason I was suspended indefinitely from everything to do with eBay. I must have done something incorrectly. They sent me an email stating that because of suspicious activity I was reviewed and was no longer a desirable customer. They were protecting their clients.

I was shocked and dismayed to the point of embarrassment. I just wanted to sell stuff and wasn't allowed to sell or purchase anything on eBay. Now what? This strange outcome made me feel at odds with my abilities. I felt like I made a sudden turn and ended up in the ditch. Now I need a tow truck or some professional help. I hope my wife won't laugh too much and help. She's got more computer experience and doesn't need to know how it happened.

Day 138 - Improvement is Possible

Why care about improving anything in retirement? It's not a product or service. I'll tell you why I do care and think we all should. Change is often described as good but that's not always true. Improvement, however, is both better and beneficial. Some of us like things to remain the same because the day-to-day experience is more comfortable.

For many of us, a challenge is not something we either desire or pursue. I consider all my activities to be challenges that I hope will help me stay healthy, wise, confident and amused. There may be some mental and physical pain involved when you challenge yourself, but as you know--no pain no gain.

What exactly do you gain? I feel with each improvement each task is more enjoyable and I find that the accomplishment makes it all worthwhile.

I play my dulcimer each week with a group for two hours. I've practiced occasionally throughout the week and only recently began to practice almost every day. I now hear the difference in my playing from how I sounded when I started, and my group appreciates my improvement. Maybe you can teach an old dog new tricks.

Day 139 - Are You A Stereotype?

I don't spend a lot of time inside my house. I like being outside and often go places and do things nearby. Many days I don't speak to many others. But when I do, I wonder how am I perceived? I bet I'm seen as a male, older guy, probably retired.

There are plenty of stereotypical views of retirees, with good reason. I most often see this when I'm driving because I do drive like an old guy which means I drive slowly. When I see a slow driver my first thought is, are they texting or speaking on the phone? Is it an older person who's retired and has all the time in the world? When I see who's driving, my response is usually, "I knew it."

Retirees are very common in Florida and many don't care about what kind of impression they are making. In most places, respect doesn't always come with age. I know I look and act like an old guy but I do my best to dispel the stereotype.

There are times when I feel like the invisible man. I do things, say things and expect things because of my age but try not to take advantage of others. I prefer to set an example. We all like to be acknowledged and common courtesies go a long way when you want something from someone. We should all be mindful when we communicate.

Day 140 - Are You Accountable?

I know I over analyze everything including retirement. My purpose is to help the reader as well as myself understand that we are transitioning into a person who for the first time in a long time has the freedom to be responsible only to themselves. Sure, your retirement affects others, but in truth you are only accountable to yourself.

I set out each day with a routine but mix things up to accommodate others. My wife will often ask what I am doing today or what I want to do over the weekend when she's not working. There are projects or chores as well as other priorities you choose. I like to question the "why" and "why not" of doing something. When I'm taking the trash out, I might tell myself, "You should wash the car." But it doesn't necessarily happen because I tell myself it's not that important yet.

I know my many character defects and will deflect, procrastinate and make mental notes throughout the day. Eventually it may no longer be possible to make excuses and I must be accountable. I like the old sayings – "practice makes perfect" and "he who hesitates is lost."

Day 141 - Leader of the Pack

I went to music class today and the two music instructors didn't show up. It's a group class and someone needed to step up and lead the class. There was a good, better and best player in class however no one seemed to want to lead or take us through the usual order of things. We somehow ended up participating in class without instruction and followed the routine we were given in previous classes. The problem I think was that we didn't learn anything and it ended up to be a class I wouldn't want to repeat.

Whether it's a group, class, game or any activity, there usually is a stated purpose, some guidelines or rules and cooperation. There's also someone or something that keeps the group in order and takes the lead. In the music class we all offered options but making a decision was difficult.

Sometimes a group consciousness decides who should step in to lead. When it doesn't, perhaps you need to be the one to rise to the occasion. Leadership is a virtue. We all have the skills, but not necessarily the confidence. Retirement might just be the time to go for it.

Day 142 - Upgrades

I think if someone offers you an upgrade, why not take it? Retirees should at least consider what's being offered and at what cost. It's a simple question, "Do you want to pay more for better? Not all upgrades are better, some are just different.

I've been considering a lot more choices now in retirement. In the past, I was always more interested in saving money, getting the deal or not fussing about more expensive options. What I bought was usually good enough. Now, however, I usually consider upgrades. It could be a car rental, hotel room, cabin on a cruise, appliances, tools and anything that I can purchase in good, better and best.

I've considered each of these recently and decided it's not just about the cost. It's time to let go of some old ideas like, "I don't need that" or "Why spend the money that way." Sure, I have a budget or idea of cost but in most cases the upgrade is desirable and I don't need to deny myself of something just to be frugal.

Many retirees, including myself, are overly conscious of money and value. The salesmen will show you the best first so you can compare lesser options from there. Experience tells me that retirement is the time to enjoy. The more experience you have, the more knowledge you will attain.

Day 143 - Going Fishing

I don't do a lot of things anymore because they don't make sense to me like they used to or I've done them before and want to do other things in retirement. I was asked to go fishing and said, "No thanks." I like fishing. I used to go fishing and didn't mind whether or not I caught anything because it was nice to be out in nature.

I wondered why I said no so quickly. I like to be on the water, getting up early is fine and traveling some distance is ok too! My conclusion was that I was not a catch and release fisherman. I didn't want to do something that didn't serve a purpose I found worthwhile. I waste a lot of time that's for sure. I drive two hours to a special beach instead of going to one that's only a half hour away. I've made this same decision when we go out to eat.

My decisions are based on desire and purpose. To what length or effort will I go to get what I want? I remember going crabbing once, spending most of the morning setting traps and freezing. When we returned the traps, the outfitter had a refrigerated case of freshly caught crabs for sale. I exclaimed to my buddy, "You mean we didn't have to catch our own crabs?" He told me "That's not the point." We had a lot to talk about on the way home but we never got around to discussing when we would go crabbing again.

Day 144 - Touch Ups

How much do retirees notice? As I was going out today my wife suggested I get some paint to touch up the walls. I didn't know how I would match the color without cutting out a piece of the wall. I also wondered what we needed to be concerned about. I didn't have any excuses because I worked in the paint department of a home improvement store and am an expert at color matching.

What I needed to find out was where were these touch up places. She quickly showed me where each wall needed to be touched up. Not only hadn't I been paying attention, but looking closely now, revealed that all of these areas were in plain sight. Maybe I didn't want to see them.

After getting the right color and touching up the spots I started to notice the trim boards also needed to be touched up. I already had the paint for that so why not make the time for further improvements? I also noticed when I was getting the paint from the garage that I should wash my car. Seems like one thing leads to another. You'll be better off paying more attention in retirement because if you don't someone else will.

Day 145 - Let the Old Folks Speak

I went to a dinner party with some young, middle-age and older folks. All the attention was given to a young couple that married two years ago. The wife was pregnant and they just recently purchased their first home. This experience brought most of us back many years and we smiled at each other as they spoke.

Nostalgically, we all asked them questions we had asked ourselves long ago. It was fun to listen and watch them respond to the questions and to each other. They were assured by all of us of the excitement, challenges, opportunities and rewards ahead of them. Then the conversation switched to the older retired folks, like me. We had been married more than forty years, our children were older than them and our comments reflected the many wonderful things in life. Be humble, show gratitude, be compassionate, show empathy and other advice was given. The need to be honest, open-minded and willing was the wisdom we all tried to pass on.

Finally, the conversation shifted to the oldest couple who had been married more than sixty years. They had been retired more than twenty years and their love for one another was still very evident. Much to my surprise, the young couple volunteered to wash the dishes.

Although they might not have been interested in what the 80-year-old's have to say, the rest of us were. The generational range was nice to experience.

Day 146 - Focus

I played pickleball again today and won the first three games. That's never happened and now I know why. Many times, I just go through the motions of organizing, planning, practicing, reviewing and expelling mental and emotional energy. But today my little accomplishment happened because I was focused.

In my case, I don't find it easy and it rarely happens enough to be noticeable. I focus more when I'm driving a car or watching a movie. I think retirement has me slowing down, not rushing and paying more attention. Being able to focus and concentrate on a task takes practice as well as a desire.

Now that I have discovered the cause and effect of staying focused, I want to apply this to build other skills. I'm far from an egomaniac but when you taste victory and feel like the effort was worth it, it's more desirable and sweeter!

My next domestic task will be to paint the front of the house. I want to start and not quit until I am done which means three days of focused work. If I can practice focusing on one task, I know my wife will be happy. I never understood the multitasking abilities some people have.

Day 147 - Windy

I love when it's windy because it's an opportunity to go windsurfing or sailing. There are other considerations before I set out on an excursion but it starts with the wind. I'm reminded of some song lyrics I heard, "You can't have a flame without a fire and you can't have a fire without desire." Sometimes I complain there isn't enough wind and other times I may say there is too much wind. The best thing I could say would be to take advantage of each day in retirement with what you have, take what you've been given and don't make excuses.

You know what they say, "Excuses are like assholes, everyone has one and they all stink." I've met some food snobs, music snobs, rich snobs, poor snobs and even wind snobs. I'm sure I've also been a snob a time or two. It doesn't accomplish anything and no one really cares about what you think you know. Many people may agree with you, but don't say anything to makes things worse. I rarely complain about the wind because I know it serves a purpose. There are plenty of other things people find to complain about in retirement.

Day 148 - Time and Money

We went to see a new home development that is a very big operation. More than ten thousand homes are going to be built in a huge planned community that will probably take thirty years to complete. It's more than a retirement community and includes homes from average to super deluxe. Nothing new for Florida, it's part of the trend of retirees moving to warmer climates and choosing to live in new communities with a lot to offer.

This particular site is centered around lakeside living. The seven lakes aren't large or connected. I really didn't consider moving there and thought why live somewhere that may take many years to complete? If I had a lot of money and I was younger, I might consider it. I like the fact that everything will be new but don't have a sense of how well it will turn out.

After our visit I realized so many decisions I make are about time and money. Maybe in retirement you can separate these two elements and make your decisions based on your purpose in retirement. Money has a purpose and time is what you make of it.

Day 149 - What's it Worth?

We continue to sell more of our things. We wanted to offer some of our items to our three children, but they don't have any space and probably wouldn't want them anyway. The items include artwork, glassware, collectibles, antiques and other nice things to look at.

How would you feel if you paid $100 for something and now it's only worth about $20 on eBay? We certainly got our use from these items and someone else will enjoy them. I told my wife we don't have to part with these items immediately. It's more like an excuse because they are taking up space we don't have. The problem is we can't get what they are worth and they may not be appreciated if they are donated.

A lot of retirees are in this situation and leave the downsizing to their heirs who just want to settle their parent's estate. Retirees who are reasonable will continue to downsize and remain in control of what happens to their possessions. Don't worry so much about what they're worth but rather what will become of them. I once said I'd rather throw it in the trash then sell it to you at that price. I wasn't fooling.

Day 150 - Getting Involved and Staying Informed

There's some new drama with the homeowner's association in our development. Retirees are very conscious when it comes to spending more money on anything. Sometimes a call for help is a call for action. I was asked to make suggestions to the board at the next meeting. We were to send emails, photos and bring along as many people as we could to address our concerns. All this involvement was not what I had in mind during retirement.

Since I chose to live in this type of residential community, involvement is important to express what affects me. Remaining silent and uninformed is not an option. How or how much you get involved depends on how serious the problem and how passionate you are about it. I'm not an organizer but I do what I can to show my support. That's usually more than I imagined.

I'm at the "asking a lot of questions" stage. Next, as a group, we will voice our concerns and hope for a reasonable decision. When you learn who decides what and how it can affect you it reveals the truth which can be good or bad. The ball's in our court.

Day 151 - Follow the Recipe

I'm now four months into my retirement, which means I'm still a newbie. One thing I've learned is that retirement is more than just a plan or idea. It's more about creating a recipe that requires combining elements that blend together for a specific result. I committed to certain activities and have limited the menu. I've set the table to look nice and function well. I have many options to further explore, but won't move on until I decide if I like what I've created thus far. This original recipe has never been tried so I'm asking myself questions and remaining patient.

On the outside it looks good but we all know it's going to have to bake, stew, cook or maybe get basted before it's ready. My eyes are bigger than my pocketbook and that's not going to change. My retirement book is doing many things for me and it will also help you. That's of course, if you follow your own recipe. Now is the time to feast from the table of life.

Day 152 - Change of Season

I retired near the end of fall and began this observational study with many notes and conversations during the winter months. It's now spring here in Florida and it may seem like that shouldn't make much difference.

The new season has brought changes like the length of the day, sunrise and sunset, temperatures, rain. Different options and activities are more available. Whether I like it or not, change has happened, so it's time to adjust. I'm still setting the alarm for seven each day. I also grew a beard over the winter and now I think it's time for a shave. I know my wife likes that notion.

During the warmer months both here and in Iowa, where I came from, the summer experience always makes me feel younger. The cold and hibernation time spent in Iowa was one reason for the move to Florida. I do miss the change of seasons which were more dramatic in the Midwest.

I wonder how different my life would be if I retired and lived in Iowa. I'm not the snowbird type but I've seen and heard enough from those who don't want to give up the change of seasons. Once again, I have realized change is good, but improvement is better.

Day 153 - You're Fired

I have a friend who once retired and then went back to work after about four months. On the new job he got fired after about six months and was very dismayed. I asked him if he will try and find another job or call it quits. He said he wasn't sure because it took a while to get the job he lost. He also asked me what it would take to get me to go back to work.

I've never been fired and only recently had to work for someone else. I was self-employed for thirty years. He said he'd been fired before and always worked for one company or another. Neither one of us had to work but my outlook was to not work for one year and then decide on the options. I also told him that the grim reaper is out there looking for men my age. He laughed and concluded we are all different so it's up to each of us to decide what's best.

I wanted to offer some encouragement and said sometimes bad things happen for a good reason. He gave me the details of the firing but I wasn't sure if he felt bad. It seemed justified but he thought that just maybe he'd get away with it. He said he missed having a routine and getting fired wasn't the worst thing that could have happened to him. I joked again saying, "Keep the grim reaper away," and "Buy my book on retirement when it's published."

Day 154 - Morning Sun

Each morning I water my many plants and enjoy a quiet meditation. I feel the warm sun on my body and there are a lot of thoughts on my mind. The warmth is comforting and I reflect on the past, present and future. Sometimes I'll have two cups of coffee afterwards. The whole experience lasts about an hour. This quiet time in retirement keeps me calm and serene. The day unfolds with decisions on chores and scheduled and unscheduled activities.

The evening routine after dinner involves watching Jeopardy, more TV and then bed by eleven. I like to pray when I lie in bed before falling asleep. I try not to think about tomorrow. Instead I reflect on the day and review what I did and why. Thoughts of a higher power enter in because I observe a lot of the natural world during the day and am in awe of everything.

The older I get the more sentimental I become. I believe either God is in everything or God is in nothing. We all choose one or the other. My quiet time helps the body and mind stay focused. With so many challenges in retirement I'm more cautious than I ever have been. Should I put on some sunscreen to really enjoy the morning sun?

Day 155 - Preservation

I'm not too sure why I have slowed down all my tasks except when you have more time you may think about preserving energy. In the earlier days of retirement, I didn't foresee too many problems and looked forward to being more energized. Less stress meant more serenity. My son had some health issues and moved back home with us. My pickleball playing gave me knee problems. My music lessons showed me how much I didn't know.

My wife gave me some advice and made it all clearer. Practice more each day on your dulcimer, get a knee brace and love your son in his time of need. She also gave me the notion that everything in life is work so take the time to enjoy the ride.

I mostly agree with her but like to add a thing or two. In this case I told her I've never been on this particular ride with these ups and downs. She reminded me that I probably expected some ups and downs so I should be more honest with myself. There's also the acceptance that there will be challenges both seen and unforeseen so preserve your energy for what's important.

This entire conversation somehow reminded me of how my twenty-mile bike ride evolved. I had to consider the route, wind, temperature, and time of day with ample water on hand. Once I did these things, I was able to accomplish this with ease. I want my retirement to last, be fulfilling and share my experiences strengths and hopes with others. That's the simple purpose. I'm going to apply an adage I had in my picture framing business, "preservation before presentation."

Day 156 - Don't Count the Days, Make the Days Count!

I spend each day reflecting on retirement to share insights, observations and opinions and offer friendly advice based on my experiences. I have been counting the days, weeks and months to keep things in perspective. I'm on a mission with a stated purpose to gain insights and adjust to retirement.

Many days get away from me and I see time really does fly when you get older. I repeat my pattern of behavior and recognize the good and bad. I think I watch too much TV and can't seem to change that behavior. I waste time like anyone else but now I'm interested in picking what I will and will not waste time on. I have to be convinced to stand in line for dinner when we go out.

My next step is to search for the right direction to take in any activity which I find worthwhile. I've always gravitated toward the road less traveled. Why not be more expressive in all you say and do? Although I'm glad to no longer be rushed, I have begun to notice that I am putting things off with excuses that ignore the obvious.

Routine will keep me moving, mixing it up will keep it exciting. I have a stated purpose and now I've given myself a roadmap. It's as if I'm stopping to enjoy the different sights and alternate between where I am and where I want to be. Should I take that trip to California? Do I have time to start another activity? Can I afford that new car? Do I need a calculator or calendar? Luckily, I already have both.

Day 157 - Would a, Could a, Should a

I've decided the regrets you have of the past need to be forgotten in retirement. Many people like the idea of writing a memoir when they're older to share their life experience. As a reader, we learn how they survived or became rich, famous or popular.

I had a small business in Iowa for thirty years, raised a family and now I am retired in Florida. If I were to write my own memoir, I don't think it would be that interesting. I lived in Cedar Rapids during the same time that actor Ashton Kutcher and the football player Kurt Warner were around. They haven't written a memoir but I certainly would read them with interest if they did. Both of these men reached great fame and fortune.

I have an aunt who wrote about the first eighteen years of growing up between 1928 and 1946 in war-torn Europe, traveling to many countries, and surviving hostility, hunger and grief. I once asked her if she would write the story of her life after this period and she said it wasn't that interesting. I told her the first part of her life she had no control over and the second part was all based on her decisions. She said there's a lot she would a, could a and should a done.

Day 158 - Distractions and Excuses

I must be some sort of perfectionist and writing this journal has made me only half content with my retirement. I want to help everyone in retirement to learn from this experience and I want to learn from them as well. When I speak to those more experienced in retirement, I'm told to give myself a lot of time to explore this new life, all its offerings and expect the unexpected. That's good advice but is there a progress in retirement? What's the difference between important and worthwhile?

Time management, money issues, energy levels, brain power and a certain amount of focus are the daily challenges we face in retirement. For me, being more busy or less busy has been a struggle between distraction and excuse.

My wife asked me today why I hadn't been windsurfing lately. It's my favorite thing to do. I need the wind, water temperature and other factors to be optimal. But she was being observant and I needed to examine this with a truthful answer to myself. I came to the conclusion that some things I like to do with others and other things I prefer to do alone. Windsurfing alone can be risky. I guess I am apprehensive to go by myself.

When I was working, I made things happen but now I'm starting to just let things happen. It's time to change that, eliminate any distractions, stop the excuses and be more mindful. My wife also suggested that, with the time I have in retirement, it would be good for me to make some new friends!

Day 159 - A Taste of Success

I felt the sweet taste of success again today. In fact, it happened two times and it felt twice as good. In pickleball I won multiple games in a row and during music class I was assured that I would be included in our outside performances. There is progress in retirement and the investment in skill development, though much slower as we age, is still attainable.

This little bit of excitement and joy inspired me to cherish the moment. I'll continue to learn because I found two things that I was previously unfamiliar with that are now a passion. I'm simply happy just to participate and improving is an added bonus. I'm having fun. The acknowledgement from teammates and fellow musicians of the progress that I am making, and their enthusiasm are encouraging beyond my expectations.

There were some helpful comments given to me early on out of courtesy. Now I realize that they have witnessed an improvement. This has changed my attitude in a positive way and brought me to a new level. Wow! We all know it's the little things in life that make us happy. I got a taste of success in my retirement I didn't expect and not only is it sweet but I now want others to experience it as well.

Day 160 - Anger Management

I got a call from a new friend who was upset and said he had to cancel our meeting because a lot of people in our group were sick, lame or lazy. While I understood his frustration and concerns, I asked him what he thought these members would say if I repeated how he described them. His reaction was even more angry and it had gotten a hold of him to the point of ridiculousness.

I've gotten upset, angry, and even a little crazy in retirement. I just didn't know if others had similar experiences. Most retirees are calm and non-confrontational. The how, what, when, and why bothered me and I told myself not to ever allow things to escalate to this level.

When I witnessed it in someone else it was a little funny. But why should others' behavior cause this kind of response? I didn't want to be part of the problem and offered a solution. I suggested that he not cancel the meeting so that those who could attend could benefit from the agenda.

Harsh words have a way of hanging around longer and people remember them. Apologies can be made, but I don't think those of us in retirement can afford to be angry. It's not good for our health or well-being and it doesn't accomplish anything. Peace be with you!

Day 161 - Lost but Not Forgotten

I look at Facebook almost every day. I know a lot of retirees use it as a window to the world. Once in a while I'll post things that I enjoy or want others to experience. We can see and learn what others are doing or have an interest in. Most of the encounters are for family and friends. I've sought out many people that were once part of my life and wondered what had become of them and where they were now.

Today my eighth-grade girlfriend found me and I shared briefly what I've been up to. I haven't seen or heard from her for over fifty years. She told me her first husband got involved with drugs, her second husband died and she contracted West Nile virus and was forced to retire because of the illness. I wasn't ready for any of this information.

We were both originally from Chicago. She moved to the Dallas area and was making the best of the situation. We drifted apart for so many years and didn't have the least bit of interest in each other. My heart went out to her. She had family and friends to help but she told me when you find yourself in times of trouble surround yourself with beauty. I'm sure I'll probably pursue other long-lost friends and acquaintances. As much as I have shut the door on the past, people remember you for different reasons and you can never have too many friends.

Day 162 - Too Much Information

I'm not feeling well today so I decided to take it easy. I'm retired so that's not much different from my everyday experience. I spent a long time reading the newspaper. It's a routine to read the paper and now I read more than ever before. Part of me just likes to be informed and learn what I can. The other part of me thinks this is a crazy world with what's happening now?

I know of two guys who spend hours each Sunday reading the New York Times. I read the local paper Thursday through Sunday. My wife will often ask "how do you know that" or "where did you hear that?" The simple answer is, "the newspaper" which offer many topics for discussion. I've been described as a deep thinker. I think things over and conclude more than most folks and sometimes it would be better if I kept my thoughts to myself.

My wife says I'm too judgmental. My response is "I call it critical thinking." My attention span is still reasonable but I'm also guilty of contempt prior to investigation. What I've read about today in the newspaper has led me to the conclusion that there's too much information for me to make sense of it. So why bother? Who cares?

In my travels I usually have to decide if I'll be informed and familiar with where I'm going or just experience the place without much knowledge? In most cases I think too much information is better than not enough.

Day 163 - Doing Things for Others

Retirees get asked to do things for others. We've got the time, ability and know how to do so many more things during each day. I suggest you establish some categories -- like what I will, what I can and what I like to do. See how this works out first before getting too committed.

I believe the saying, "no good deed goes unpunished," is true from experience. This won't stop me from offering to help but I know to be careful. Retirement is a great time to become less self-centered and self-serving. I don't set any expectation when I offer my services. But folks you decide to help may have their own agenda. You should try to get the details. For example, someone might ask you to help them move. You might think they just need help moving furniture and boxes. They may think you are there to help them pack, move, and unpack. Are you up for it?

Your actions will be appreciated no doubt and showing concern, kindness and purpose is a reward in itself. Living life on life's terms comes with experience. We have a chance now to offer our help to others and support the things we stand for. Each day I'm retired I have a renewed sense of appreciation and want others to love life as much as I do.

Day 164 - Fat Chance and No Way in Hell!

You and I and many other retirees won't always get to hear the truth that we want. In my experience I've heard retirees say and think out loud things that they don't have a clue about. It sounds nice in conversation to express a desire to hike the Grand Canyon. But who's kidding who?

I've also heard many retirees say they are going to travel now that they're retired. When I ask what their first trip will be, there's a moment of silence followed by a brief answer. I realize they are speaking in general terms but they don't actually have a plan. Then I wonder if they have experience and money and have set a date.

I've found myself in the same situation. It is fun to think out loud and see others' reactions. Some retirees don't see or hear themselves very well. When I meet someone who is in great shape, wearing stylish clothes, and behaving in the politest manner, I begin to pay greater attention. If they have something to say and can explain it in detail then I believe them. If I begin to doubt any part of a conversational exchange, it's hard for me to continue to pay attention.

When I hear stories of travel adventures I don't care as much about where they went as what they did while there. I cannot be sure, but some grandiose responses often get me thinking, "fat chance and no way in hell do I believe them." I know myself to be practical and forthright with my adventure choices. I hope I can remain observant and distinguish between the truth of what is said and not said. Honestly, I think it is important to be honest!

Day 165 - Taxman Time

It's the middle of April and taxes are due once again. This will be the last time I will pay taxes on any working income. In retirement you will have to live within your financial means but taxes aren't going away. So far, I haven't controlled my spending like I should. I'll give myself one year to adjust to a different cashflow. In the meantime, what will I do about taxes, inflation, emergencies, other family members' needs and the never-ending question of how much money will I need in retirement?

My business accountant told me two things I've never forgotten: always pay yourself first and make more money so you can afford to pay your taxes. I always complained about paying taxes but he never budged or offered any sympathy or agreement.

Accounting and retirement are fact-based. Whether or not you can afford something is only relevant in context to your budget. I don't think I'll be speaking to him much now because I plan to make things very uncomplicated. He'd probably tell me I can do what I like but the taxman and the grim reaper will always find my door. Maybe I need his advice or at least I should thank him for all he did for me in the past. Last time we spoke he did say, "I'll see you next year."

Day 166 - Why Do You Worry?

Everyone knows that "don't worry, be happy" are just words to a popular song. I like to worry more than normal because I like the drama. I verbalize my feelings much too often. When I meet someone who worries more than me I know how my wife must feel around me.

Worry causes me and many retirees to not take action. Your inability to think and act causes others to not trust you and soon your burden becomes their burden. It's really not the way to live. If you are looking for sympathy, why not just ask for help?

Have you ever walked out of an office building, theatre or department store and wondered where you parked your car? The airport parking lot is the worst especially when you've been away for a week or more. The simple solution to this is don't give yourself a reason to worry and take steps to prevent a dilemma. A proactive approach will reduce the drama and result in both security and comfort.

It seems as if the longer I'm retired the easier it is to let others worry about their own welfare. I'm improving my confidence with these experiences and fear and worry are disappearing. It's magic!

Day 167 - Wing It

I found myself in Ft. Myers, two hours from where I live for two days without an intended purpose. My wife had some business so I went along for the ride and thought it would be fun to explore the area. I never just go to a strange town and wing it. This excursion could help my retirement experience allowing me to see how I do when I explore and familiarize myself with new sights and opportunities on my own.

I set out to see art galleries, plant nurseries, and a somewhat remote nearby island. I saw tourists and probably also retirees everywhere I went. Was I doing what these types of individuals would do? I only have two days so it's important to choose wisely. Being alone, I only had to satisfy my own curiosities.

I think I've learned another lesson in retirement. I went at my own pace, had many nice things to say about where I went but I really should have spoken to someone from this area first. I also could have done more research about the place. If your trying to wing it in retirement or have to wing it you'll benefit much more with as much information you can obtain ahead of time. Now I know why you need a wingman.

Day 168 - Catch Up to What?

I was out of town for two days, traveling in unfamiliar surroundings. Getting away is always refreshing and gives you insights into other places. Staying in a hotel makes me appreciate my home. Often, no matter how long or short the out-of-town experience is, I feel different for a few days afterward because of what I've seen and done.

Being home again I started to forget about what I didn't see or do on my trip and my attention turned to what needs to be done around here. I wanted to catch up to get back into the routine. Funny, I left to get out of the routine and now I want to get back into it. It took all day to get back to normal. By six at night I seemed to forget I had ever left.

This experience has taught me that I must need some excitement in retirement but I also need my routine. Anything new takes some adjustment. Anything different takes understanding. If you're a retiree like me you'll probably like it when things get back to normal. But it's good to savor the excitement, so don't rush to catch up.

Day 169 - Sail Away!

It's near the end of April and I've only gone sailing once this year. That was last month, but I love sailing and would like to go more often. Today my wife and I will sail away with our dog Scrappy. Last night I was at the sailing club pizza party and earlier got the boat ready. Being near the sailing site two days in a row was a reminder of how much I enjoy the activity and all that goes into it.

I know why I haven't done it sooner and more often. I only sail with a partner and that happens to be my wife. She is still working and will be for the near future. Her interest in sailing brought her to conclude that I needed a sailing buddy so I could go out more often.

I think of sailing as a short vacation with four parts--preparation, the actual experience, clean up and repacking, and discussing the day's events. I actually met a fellow sailor today who was having trouble getting out to the water. We exchanged phone numbers and I hope for the best. On the way home I thought about when I will be able to go sailing again? I should make this happen more often in retirement.

Day 170 - Trivia Games

I watch Jeopardy as much as I can which is almost every day and have done so even before I retired. I'm certainly not very smart but I usually answer at least ten to thirteen questions correctly. If they gave you more time, I bet I could answer two or three more questions, but not more than that. The reason why I like it so much is because I learn what I don't know and am surprised at what I do know.

The information, familiarity, knowledge, and memory skills amaze me. Some people really get into trivia and play at local bars. I'm retired and though I really don't need to be reminded of how much I know or don't know, can't remember, never knew or don't care to know, I like the excitement and I do learn more about the world.

Watching trivia on TV or playing games in your home or in bars tells you a lot about each individual that chooses to play. Retirees like all kinds of games and it keeps the mind sharp. We all only know what we know but it's up to us to discover more.

Day 171 - New Clothes and a New Attitude

I decided to take my pickleball playing up a notch and get some new sportswear. Since I was shopping for clothes anyway, why not a complete spring ensemble to upgrade my appearance on the playing field. New clothes always improve my attitude, and I like to think, also helps my playing ability. If it doesn't change my game it still looks good and I feel better.

Comfort and style were never my main concerns with clothes. During my retirement I always thought I would become more stylish. Whenever I see retirees with new apparel and the latest styles, I think good for them and why not enjoy fashion? We not only set an example but it shows we are paying attention and like to be active in many pursuits.

In formal settings it's often a show to see what people wear. I won't judge a book by its cover but it does catch my attention. The first impression you make may be due to your clothes. Most of the pickleball players wear sportswear with bright and colorful themes. I bought some outfits and my playing partner immediately noticed and gave me a compliment. I looked more professional and the outfit said I was serious and prepared to compete. I'm not sure if my opponents felt the same.

Day 172 - All in Good Time

As my wife nears retirement, two weeks away, we started to pencil in some options for travel and exploration in the surrounding area. We've been here in Florida almost five years and said we'd explore the area first before we ventured out to far off places. Moving to our retirement spot and continuing to work gave us time to adjust. Many retirees like to explore different areas and soon decide where they might go.

Almost every retiree we meet is from somewhere else and we quickly learn how we each ended up here? Moving to a retirement spot away from home is not without reservation. Many people I know have family and friends they would never consider leaving. Our first step to move was to make the move. Next, we got acquainted with our new surroundings and started a life different from the one we had. The third step was to take advantage of the old adage "enjoy the early years of retirement while your health and abilities are still strong."

While we lived in Iowa for thirty years, we somehow didn't have the time to see much of the state. We've told ourselves many times that retirement had come at a good time; we'll both be 64. We are anticipating being able to spend more time with family and friends and offer a great winter retreat to our Midwest visitors.

Our gratitude attitude continues to grow as does our appreciation for retirement. It's time to plan a trip.

Day 173 - So Long

It happened for the second time recently -- I had to say so long to a new acquaintance. Two retirees I know changed their mind about where they decided to retire. I've said it a lot to friends and family that Florida is not for everyone. I'd never heard a complaint from these two folks about moving here or what they didn't like or needed to have to be happier.

Their experience of a year taught them that what was once important has now changed. I asked if it was friends or family, weather, cost of living or something specific that they were missing. They said that they just didn't like the Florida summers. Even though I only knew them a short time, it was going to be hard to say good-bye. I was hoping we'd become better friends.

I was immediately surprised to hear the news because I'd never thought that many retirees move more than once. In each case the move wasn't going to be back home but to somewhere else. The fact that retirement may not be your last move became clear to me. Saying good-bye doesn't get any easier.

Day 174 - Unusual People

I decided after many years of observing my fellow men and women that although those who were unusual had obvious virtues and faults, they didn't let that stop them from being who they were or who they wanted to be. I start out trying to be polite, encouraging, and helpful. I'll also make excuses, get complacent, self-serving and even wonder why I behave this way or that.

I think retirees begin living their new life with an unrealized purpose and it's a time of adjustment and discovery. My wife told me as soon as she retires, she would like to find out more about herself. She wants to explore her feelings. She knows I really identified with my job and all it had to offer. It was hard for me to let go of the past but I immediately gave myself the new job of staying healthy.

She thought that's a great idea and reminded me that I could do more than that. Retirement may last many years so why not relax and give yourself more time to explore and discover. As a male I don't necessarily agree, because males don't live as long as females, they behave differently and want things to happen sooner rather than later.

I think of myself as amusing and I like to be funny. I even stated I'd like to try stand-up comedy. The fact that I said this is not unusual, but if I actually do it, that would be.

Day 175 - Toxic

It's all in the name of fun. Booze, drugs, babes, food, gambling, fun in the sun and many other recreational activities are a retiree's choice. I mention this because I have witnessed such behavior, and while not too surprised, I do wonder what they were thinking? Time and money to spend, restaurants, bars, casinos, malls, resorts, cruises and many other stimulating experiences can entice just about anyone.

Partaking in any of these activities is the good life we hear about and they are definitely fun. They all offer some form of escape from reality and many retirees like to be entertained. Without the constraints of working a job comes a lot more time for pleasure seeking than we are used to and that can be toxic.

Moderation is the obvious solution but it's easier said than done. I've already gained some weight in retirement and it's not from a sedentary lifestyle, but rather a love of food and going out. I get a lot of offers in the mail and online to spend time and money to see and do things. During my retirement it's hard to say how much of a good time is a good time.

A recent dinner guest asked us if we ever smoked marijuana and if we'd mind if she did. She said she only smoked a very little each day for recreation and it did her good. Saying no thanks to the offer was all it took, but if you decide to partake in these types of activities, just ask yourself, "What is your motive?" Judging yourself is worthwhile and judging others is toxic.

Day 176 - Continue to Search

The music group I belong to that meets once a week has a founding leader who is very particular about every aspect of the class, including practice and attendance. If you miss a class, she'll let you know. I happen to appreciate her candor and how she runs the group.

During her own absence one week, I found out that there was another group that had formed that played at the same time but on another day at another location. I found out not everyone liked our group leader's way of conducting practice and would like to change to another format. I'm not qualified to speak, having only been part of the group for a short time.

I wouldn't leave this group and I'm not willing yet to be part of two groups. For me this would be over extending myself. I was offered this information and invitation and wondered if I would be judged for my dedication and loyalty.

Should I continue to search for more or better opportunities? All of us in the group have been retired for different lengths of time and have varying amounts of music experience and skill.

I like when things become familiar. Some retirees must just like variety and others like change. The leader made it very clear early on that it was because of her 50-plus years of teaching and playing music, that her way was the best way to learn. Each of us will eventually decide for ourselves, but right now I choose to make the best of what I have. Perhaps, in the future I will continue to search for other opportunities.

Day 177 - Let's Not Argue

I think I'm more open-minded in retirement. I've experienced a lot of changes in my surroundings and the people in my life. Not everything is working in my sketchy master plan. Many of my decisions and their merits were not always clear. I've argued with myself and others to support my position but my arguments also were not always very clear.

I've noticed a division in the old versus young in retirement. They both argue each and every point the same but the conclusion from the old is you'll see when you get there. The more recently retired trust the more experienced retirees but think it will be different for them. It seems like a generational divide as in previous decades and age groups.

I'd much rather listen to these folks than argue with younger inexperienced peers. I usually say let's not argue because the other folks don't know what we know and we don't know what they know. We are both trying to help each other improve our lives. We trust each other because we've learned what matters in retirement. The conversation doesn't end with we agree to disagree. Instead, we express our knowledge rather than opinion. You'll always learn more when you listen than when you speak.

Day 178 - Sensitive Seniors

In a small group discussion today, I sensed two of the participants were overly sensitive to suggestions, opinions and some random observations. Do we become more sensitive in our older age? Do retirees have to protect or defend themselves and express their rights?

Retirees need to become familiar with retirement. Some retirees I've spoken with at length need to learn to express what they've always felt but could never articulate. Their new-found freedom was earned in different degrees and came at different times in their lives. Some are ready for it, some are not.

One woman told me her husband couldn't wait to retire so he could play more golf. He now plays more golf but his game hasn't improved and neither has his attitude. You can very easily get caught up in the adjustment to retirement and become overly sensitive.

If you recognize these folks, it's probably because you were once like them. I think of myself as emotional and sensitive and can easily get hurt feelings. This can lead to either passive-aggressive behavior or withdrawal from people. It's time to act your age.

Day 179 - Hurt Feelings

My wife noticed I wasn't very motivated today and asked if I was feeling ok? I told her about some sensitive retirees and the conversations we had yesterday. This experience made me rethink how I should speak and present myself to others.

I may have hurt some feelings and we all know what that feels like. Retirees are always adjusting to change like everyone else but they also give themselves the benefit of the doubt. In the past their careers, family's well-being, positions and social standing in the community were at risk based on their behavior and comments.

Retirees like to say and do what's on their mind. We've all heard our grandparents shout out some funny and bold statements. Our mental states may have changed with age but I think the freedom to express pent-up emotion can lead to some embarrassing moments and hurt feelings.

Retirees also don't get over things quickly. We need time to rethink the situation and then realize the effect we have with our words and actions. I'll seek advice and counsel to get things back to normal. It won't hurt to be nice!

Day 180 - Time Away

Many of my fellow retirees are planning and going on vacation to some far-off places. When you're retired do you need a vacation or just time away? My wife and I are doing both but not to any far-off place. What's made it exciting is she is finally retiring and we are planning to meet up with family to share a beachside home for one week. It's part celebration, part vacation and start of our new life in retirement.

I've been retired for six months to the day and haven't been away for a week or more since our trip two years ago to Crete. Each and every trip has created new memories of some unique experiences. The excitement of going away is worth all the planning and worries of leaving home. Each detail of going away reminds me that no matter how much you plan there will always be some unexpected situation.

I like being in new surroundings. It gives me a new perspective on life and keeps me living in the present. I also feel more part of the greater whole of mankind. Our relationships, age and abilities define us. Retirees are unique because they can spend a lot of time living in the present which allows them the chance to share their experiences with zeal and zest. All this happens because we often get more time away.

Day 181 - Ducks in a Row

With guests coming and going and planning our vacation, we've spent a lot of time preparing. When I recall similar times, I'm quickly reminded of how everything was last minute. Now that I'm retired, I think I'll try to get things done on time with little or no stress.

Making the effort versus thinking things through are different approaches. I don't think retirees like to put too much on their plate. But, more time on their hands should give retirees the chance to step back and get a clear perspective.

I've second-guessed myself so often and have asked, did I forget something I planned to bring, or not even remember to put it on the list? I know I've never been well organized at home or work but too many details will slow you down.

The way to expedite is get those ducks in a row with a priority list. It's that simple and there is no need to falter. Ask for help, delegate and realize there are supervisors, peers and subordinates just like when you were working. My advice would be to say thank you as often as necessary.

Day 182 - Love the One You're With

I continue to appreciate almost everything in retirement and don't take it for granted. It's that time in your life when people, places and things begin to pass and you don't like it. I have to work at not getting depressed. My technique is to make myself available in thought and action as well as think of how others are doing.

One of the hardest things for me to do is to continually be of service to others. I don't do it enough and when I'm willing and able I immediately feel better. My conclusion has been I'm self-centered and self-serving. I once thought maybe I was just needy. Being needy in retirement should be avoided at all costs because no one likes this kind of behavior.

I like the expression, "Fake it until you make it." It gives you time to balance the needs of others with your own. Loving those around you can help you develop a new way of approaching life with rewards both now and later. Retirement has a way of forcing you to ask yourself if you've done the right thing. What will you say?

Day 183 - Encouragement

I love to give and receive encouragement. There exists a life force in all of us, particularly retirees, that wanes, gets lost and needs to be re-awakened. Today I would like to practice what I preach, do what I say, and eliminate every little bit of BS.

I've received many kind remarks about my musical abilities, sports play, and beautification around the house from my spouse and others. It doesn't matter too much where it comes from as long as it's from someone you respect and admire and is honest. Sometimes I think I need more encouragement as a retiree than when I was a kid. Back then I didn't know any better and took things for granted. Now I know that today, tomorrow and next week will be better if I can offer a kind word and accept life on life's terms.

Day 184 - Good Time

We went on a vacation to have a good time. I've met a lot of retirees who have gone on several trips every few months to enjoy all the wonderful places they have never seen but hoped to. Being retired frees up the spirit of adventure. Why not live it up with a good time?

We plan to go on a variety of trips that will be both new and exciting. For some reason sunsets in different places with different folks are just better. How often do you at a chosen time sit and watch an event that happens every day whether you're paying attention or not?

When I was in the picture framing business, I can't tell you how many photos of sunsets I framed. Usually, each and every time the customer was in awe as they placed the photos in front of me to also admire. I would acknowledge their beauty and ask where the photos were taken? Before they answered I often heard how they had a good time on vacation and were really glad to have taken these photos. Good times will happen in many ways in retirement but you will have to be ready when and where they happen.

Day 185 - Family vs. Friends

We rented a big house while on vacation and invited both family and friends to join us. Each family member has a special role or position in our lives and our friends came along to share in this experience.

I've met retirees who never like to bring these two groups together. Family comes first and certainly occupies a lot of our time and effort. During retirement both of these groups may seem to be more outspoken. As we look out for each other's needs the retirees will want to feel more safe, secure, cared for and respected than ever before.

Our families may not know us as well as our friends. While on this vacation we will undoubtedly renew our roles and share in the moment which can help us grow closer and feel like family. I think retirees need to continue to seek friendships and at the same time make the relatives comfortable and loved. If you ever wonder how you got to where you are it may have been because of family and friends. Both are important and have contributed to the way you play the game of life.

Day 186 - Shared Experiences

As the vacation progresses and days pass, we soon learn that those of us who are retired definitely have a different outlook and attitude about each day. We are with a majority of folks who are coming and going according to their planned vacation time, work schedule and have their own expectation of the shared experience.

I've driven to the airport three times with three groups coming and going. Each group upon arrival expressed their excitement for the week. The same goes for the good-byes and expressing sorrow when it's time to leave. I get sentimental and tell them "don't be sad it's over, be glad it happened." I always get some "aaah's." The shared experience is so wonderful that we all feel it may never happen again and have made the most of each moment together.

What I like to do before our guests leave is to start a discussion about where and when we can get together next. As a retiree, you don't have to be the organizer. But as a senior, I suggest you assume this role and try it out. Sometimes all you have to do is call it a reunion. For me, dining or watching a sunset alone can be nice. But sharing the experience with others, always makes it better.

Day 187 - What Are You Going to Do?

I met a friend of a friend on vacation who joined us for dinner. He moved to Florida and lives on a boat. He's old enough to retire but said many times during the evening, "What am I going to do?" I know there are many of retirement age who are almost ready to retire but either can't or don't want to let go of a schedule, purpose or activity that they enjoy.

I certainly understand that money matters, but I try to encourage them to decide what's most important at this time in their lives. The transition from old life to new life can be gradual. You can explore many options and nothing is set in stone.

Before my wife and I retired we discussed the fact that this may not be our last move. What we do now may not be what we do next. Our new friend who's lived on his boat for five years has a girlfriend who simply won't live on the boat. He told me it may soon come to either the boat or girlfriend. I wished him luck and said his girlfriend looked better than the boat and had more to offer. He gave me a nervous laugh and realized what choice I'd make.

Day 188 - How About Going Jet Skiing?

Wow! It's a great rush to go out on the Gulf of Mexico, full throttle, waves rolling, water spraying, planning and then propelling out of the water for a brief moment on a jet ski. Being retired makes me want to try new things.

I think my friends and family are a little surprised that someone my age is willing and able to try exciting things that I've never done before. I know my limits and they are rapidly changing but I won't stop until I have to.

I've spent my life trying to be able to maintain my abilities. Many retirees aren't as lucky because they never really did much as a younger person to preserve their physical capacity. Now that I have started to play pickleball, I wish I would have discovered it sooner.

I believe that some retirees can do more than they think. You just have to set a limit on each new experience or activity. My wife and I went kayaking twice in one week. The first place was challenging but yesterday's trip was slow, easy going and not very long or far. I would tell retirees to never say never but to be realistic and approach new thrills with caution.

I completely understand that some activities just aren't a person's cup of tea. For me, it's amusement park rides. Even though I know they are safe, the rush and thrill don't surpass the wooziness I feel afterward. As I left the water's edge today, I wondered what I would be willing to try next?

Day 189 - Right in the Middle

It's midweek during our vacation and I don't have to worry about what's waiting for me back at work. Being retired and on vacation is the best. This midweek observation is a good reminder for me that what I've done and what I'd like to do next are really my only concerns.

Being all right and feeling content sometimes requires looking backward and forward at the same time. I know some retirees don't get concerned about what was or what's going to be. They feel all right all the time and don't waste time or energy on too much planning. I've only recently learned about the proper placement of expectations.

As I was writing this journal I was approached by a recent retiree. It was early morning and I was sitting on the beach. Within ten minutes I exchanged and received information, made a friend, offered encouragement and shared a common bond. This was followed by a handshake from someone I know I will never see again.

I now wonder if this vacation and the time being retired has changed me. I know I'm more open and friendly but I don't think I would have engaged with him to this extent and approached him as he did me if I wasn't feeling so good this morning. Sometimes things happen for a reason and I'm enjoying the good time. If you are recently retired, a vacation might just be what you need to make you feel better about the world. Talking to a stranger may also help.

Day 190 - You Can Get What You Want

I don't want to limit myself in retirement. I've always lived with a realistic view but as I look back on the past, I don't want it to define my future. I say a lot of things and appear to be willing to participate in new adventures. But sometimes the things I want, places to see, and experiences to have are just ideas that pass through my mind. I'm trying to be accountable for each step I take and word I speak.

Throughout her life, my mother continued to tell me, "You made your bed now sleep in it." As a retiree, I've started to question this expression as well as others I heard growing up. "Turn the other cheek," is another one. I'm having a difficult time just accepting these adages at face value. Since we only know what we know it's up to us to question some of the things we've just accepted up until now. Maybe there are other options to explore.

If you're retired, soon to be retired or want to be sort of retired think about each action you take as the beginning of a new life. What you do or don't do from here on out is going to be viewed by others as what you did in retirement.

This little wisdom that's my own and not borrowed I'm happy to share and will even discuss in the following pages. I've passed the sixth month mark of retirement and wonder what else I want? Can I get it? Why or why not? Time will tell and you won't need a watch to find out.

Day 191 - New Transitions

Vacation is now over. It's the first time for me to return from a week of fun and adventuring without worrying about going back to work. There's still the home chores and other responsibilities to attend to but I have the option to relax and make the transition back to the routine at my desired pace.

Each time I get back to my routine I see how I feel first and then I decide on what works for me. I've gotten some new ideas on the last vacation and though I'm full of excitement, I need to make note of the insights I learned from this past one. I was eager for each activity we chose and my main concern throughout the planning was not to miss the best of all there was to see and do.

My wife and I knew there would be some compromising and others needs and wants had to be considered. There was one day in which no one wanted to do anything except relax on the beach or poolside. I surprised everyone as the retired guy who didn't want to relax and had other ideas. I went along with the group and enjoyed many conversations. I tried to be the best host I could be and many times I was told retirement had made me a new man. I was energized and so hospitable it was appreciated and amused many of the guests.

I told everyone that in retirement you have fewer things to worry about and can enjoy your new found freedom. If you don't have too much on your plate it's easier to make each transition with a gratitude attitude. It's your retirement and you will continue to learn how to best navigate it by appreciating each moment.

Day 192 - Never the Less

I've noticed that many retirees like improvements and expect things in retirement to be better than what they were before. Our time and cash limits dictate many options but our new status of being retired makes us reassess who we are, what we have and why we have it.

We may choose to eliminate some excesses, simplify our day-to-day and start to adjust to what's really important to each of us. It is up to us to decide how and with whom we spend our time and money. I don't think we need to compare ourselves because there are many variables that can shape retirement differently for each of us.

I know I can and should do with less. I've realized there's no reason to wait. Whenever I made changes in the past, I usually came around to saying what was I waiting for? My wife often shared with me her philosophy of never wish less for others but more for yourself. She wasn't always speaking about material things either.

I see myself as husband, father, brother, uncle, nephew, neighbor and friend. I know I have room to improve in each of these roles and will continue to do so in retirement, as these relationships are vital to my happiness.

I've known some hard-driving aggressive males that have turned into kind compassionate fellows after a short time in retirement. When they transitioned from working in the material world, they became more spiritual and began to place greater value on their relationships with others. I think retirees learn that they can begin to do more and ask for less.

Day 193 - Won't You Join Me?

Today my wife will join me in retirement. I've waited six months for her new status and wonder how much I'll say about what I've learned and what she should expect in retirement. The transition will take time so I've decided to have a wait and see attitude. We each had different expectations coming home from vacation this week. My routine and her yet to be developed routine will start to challenge us and may redefine mine.

There is the yours, mine and ours of a marriage or relationship. I don't expect her to do much of anything I'm doing. If you asked me what will draw her interests and where will they be, I'd tell you that I don't really know, but I'm anxious to find out. It took me months of discovery, trial and error and a lot of soul searching to find out what was worthwhile for me.

As she discovers her course of action, I hope we can find something we can share. Having spent a lifetime together we will have to approach our retirement as a discovery for us individually and as a couple. If this sharing aspect doesn't happen right away that's ok, too. I know if I go fishing, she would rather go to a yoga class. I told her today I don't remember my first day of retirement. She responded with, "Why would you"? Each morning now we have coffee time. We chat about the day.

Day 194 - Rainy Days and Mondays

I've got both a Monday and a rainy day today, with rain expected all week. When I was a kid, rainy days were the worst time because I was stuck inside the house. I feel the same way today except there's no one to complain to or give me advice.

My wife had plans and is gone for the day. I happen to have alternative plans for rainy days so it's not that bad. I do realize that I must plan ahead if it's going to be like this for the next four days. In retirement changes don't occur just because of weather, there are a lot of opportunities with the people you interact with to consider. This is the time I ask what others are doing and have I considered all the options?

If you engage in a conversation or encounter, you might come up with some new options to consider. If I sit here on the lanai and watch the rain all day, I might get depressed. If I do this for the next four days, I might go crazy.

The solution is always to plan ahead and not take things for granted. Foreseeing the future is not necessary but having a Plan B is a good idea and even a Plan C and D. I even slept a little longer today because of the gloomy weather. Even with a good plan in place, circumstances can still get in your way. The expression, "If you are given lemons make lemonade," is appropriate but I think planning a nice meal tonight is a better idea. I guess I'm going to the grocery store.

Day 195 - Not So Fast

Are retirees quick to judge? What's best for me? What's going to happen if I do or don't do something? It's one of those nagging questions days. My wife's first day of retirement and her thoughts on it are probably of more concern to me than her.

I'm writing this journal to help myself and others to learn of the experience and define their retirement as a new way of life. She is doing and acting in a way that I find predictable based on observations. I've reminded myself to not be so fast to judge what she chooses to do during her first week or first month because I'm not an expert, but rather an observer and reporter.

My preparations were based on me being ready and willing to retire. That's the first step. Second step is taking action. Step three is to review the results and pursue a level of satisfaction which should take precedence. That's my current approach. "Easy does it" is my mantra. Others will have completely different ideas and that's understandable.

Many retirees will feel like they can break free, expand their interests, and be spontaneous, having little concern for the outcome. Those of you who are not sure whether to jump in or take your time, let me assure you that to find more things to consider, you just have to start looking.

It may take me this whole week to get back to my pre-vacation routine. The vacation hasn't faded from my mind but I know it will. Before it does, I'm going to plan something for the weekend. There's more than one lane on the highway of life and switching lanes is ok. The fast lane has its purpose but so does the slow lane. Which one's for you?

Day 196 - Morning, Noon and Night

Most retirees begin and end their day within their preferred timeframe. I get up at seven no matter what. Bedtime is by 11 PM. I've accepted my current schedule, but will continually work to improve or refine it to suit my needs.

Sometimes I'll be idle drinking coffee and enjoying the sunrise. I've been writing this journal in the mornings and reflecting on yesterday or planning today. I'm consistent with what I choose to do morning, noon and night. Our habits do define our state of mind and we occupy ourselves based on our way of life.

Do you take a shower in the morning or at night? Do you eat more in the first half or second half of the day? I may be more regimented than I think. If it's eleven in the morning and I haven't had coffee or breakfast I probably will skip it and look toward lunch.

In retirement I've come to enjoy more time more than anything, but I feel a bit of guilty if it gets out of hand. A three-hour lunch is somewhat excessive. I have lowered my expectations for serenity sake and doing things in a timely manner is still a priority.

I have to be careful not to deflect, justify or fall back on excuses like saying, "I'm retired and can do whatever I want." I like the expression, "Yesterday's history, tomorrow's a mystery, so accept the present we call today." I think I'll get another cup of coffee right now. My morning break isn't over yet.

Day 197 - Economy of Motion

In my dulcimer music class, we reviewed economy of motion. I wasn't surprised it existed but rather why we didn't learn about it sooner. I've moved along so far in retirement free spirited, content and open to suggestions. I've explored many options and reduced any stress with my "don't worry be happy attitude."

When I'm playing music, the flow is a variable based on my skill and understanding of the notations. I can use my thumb, but others either can't or won't. But I have difficulty with timing. We all compensate for a variety of reasons to accomplish our goals. Each of us learns at a different pace and plays at a different level.

I'm going to apply this notion of economy of motion in retirement. I'm determined to not waste time or money. These two concerns are present each day and even if I had more of each, I think it is important to budget both aspects to keep things under control.

A friend of ours spent the night at our home because we live closer to the airport. She wanted a shorter commute because she had to get up very early and didn't want to drive for hours upon waking. When she first made the request, I thought it was strange and I probably wouldn't have thought about the drive time. Now however, I do see that the economy of motion is worthwhile. Doing what's best, easier and in some ways safer is something to think about in retirement.

Day 198 - Trial and Error -- Part 2

"What are you doing now with those plants of yours," my wife curiously asked. I spend a lot of time with my plants. I've got many orchids and other exotics that I call specimens. I easily spend an hour each day caring for them. After coming back from vacation, I had to do some catching up, repotting, trimming, manicuring and watering a little extra. I'm not an expert, but I've had plants in my life for thirty years and gardening is my passion. I have made many mistakes but never worried too much. I like to experiment and see what happens.

My sister-in-law recently said I was doing my retirement right. My response was "Thanks, I think you're right because I do many things that have more than one purpose." She appreciated seeing all the beautiful flowers in bloom and can see I've continued to pursue my interest in plants during retirement.

During her recent visit she said she noticed a difference in my personality and wondered was it something that came with retirement or did I just change. I told her that my plants and my retirement both involved some trial and error. If something doesn't work in retirement or one of my plants doesn't thrive, I learn from the experience and try not to worry too much.

I think a lifetime of working at a job does affect everyone to a different degree. I feel freed up now and am open to discovery which is part of the fun. Her situation is different than mine. She is not in a position to retire completely but would like to transition to part-time and work as long as she can.

That's a great idea that I had also thought of. Each of us needs to ask the same questions of how, what, when and why. When I paid off the home mortgage and announced my retirement many people congratulated me and said that it was an accomplishment. It's something to be proud of just like the flowers I planted and the decisions I made about retirement. It has been a trial and I did error some, but it has definitely been worth it.

Day 199 - Get the Ball Rolling

Retirement isn't a game. But it can be a lot of fun.

I like some games more than others because of how well I do and how much I can participate. I play pickleball two or three times a week and look forward each time I get ready for a match. All the games are mixed doubles with a variety of skill levels. Everyone who participates is appreciated and we encourage each other to a great degree.

Between games we talk about our retirement and detail what we've done, what we are planning to do, including any travel plans, restaurant experiences, golf and kayaking adventures. We have sons and daughters, grandchildren and even moms and dads to contend with but each of us sees the challenges as normal and part of life. We set out to meet others by participating in sports, card games and so many other activities retirees can do.

We got the ball rolling and help each other in our many pursuits. The encouragement, recognition and group dynamics is the best reward with so many laughs and good times. We do keep score but it's only for one day and our main goal is to keep the ball rolling. These insights can also be applied to retirement.

Day 200 - Appearances

I grew a beard when I retired and decided to shave it off on Mother's Day. There wasn't a particular reason for doing either one. I've gotten many reactions to my new appearance but not everyone responded and many times it took longer than I thought for any comments to be made.

My wife likes to go to the gym often and goes for health and beauty benefit. One of the first things she did in retirement was to start going to an exercise class. I think most retirees care about their appearance, and health is a concern for all of us. But some use their retirement status as an excuse when they say, "Who cares what I look like?"

Some retirees claim no one looks at them anyway. I've heard them say, "What's the difference?" I think I've felt this way often as well. It takes effort like everything else and you need to continue to remind yourself that all that you do, all that you say, how you do it and even what you wear when this happens is a reflection of the inner you.

Often your outward appearance is a manifestation of your current state of mind. I'm more or less not overly concerned about my appearance but I greatly admire those who look good and show they care. I often say I want to improve my day-to-day appearance but have only on occasion tried to be more conscientious. I even fantasized about being a classy dresser when I retired. I'm working on it. I think of it as an improvement. Who can argue with "Change is good, but improvement is better?"

Day 201 - Turn Regrets into Resets

Once in a while I hear someone say they have no regrets. I've had them and continue to form new ones. In these last few months of retirement I wanted to avoid this as much as possible. I have enough from the past.

My solution is to reset my thinking. I've reset clocks, computers, phones and other things with a purpose to make them right and work properly. I've realized that many times there's more than one solution to a problem. I also believe it's expected that retirees will ask for help when they need it. A second opinion may stop the regret from having a chance to set in.

I've bought some things in retirement and I don't have any regrets about objects but rather choices. Most of my regrets have to do with not taking action as opposed to taking action. What I said, did or didn't do and when this or that should have been done are part of my daily thoughts.

Having the notion of a reset in retirement gives you the chance to improve your situation. When other things in your life don't work you can fix or replace them. If you're not happy with yourself or a situation make an amend and think of it as a reset. Retirement is a gift that keeps on giving; you just have to make sure it continues to work.

Day 202 - When You are Both Retired

It doesn't always happen at the same time. Retirement happened to me six months ago and my wife has been retired for one week. Her experience and mine are similar but not the same. I've actually been studying, reading and speaking with retirees with the purpose of this journal in mind. I've also tried to interpret the many choices we make.

We don't know what we as a couple will do together and though it's been discussed it's really up in the air. Individually we are taking time to explore and experiment with the options and suggestions we hear about. My wife has offered me suggestions and I offer her my occasional insight.

We continue to maintain our home and previous interests as we have in the past. I still mow my own lawn and paint my own house. Some retirees hire others to do these types of things. I'm not there yet.

We are preoccupied with our daughter's wedding which will happen at the end of the year and will hopefully visit some relatives soon. We understand each other's schedules and look forward to more shared experiences. I've been talked into a yoga class before and may join in others in the future. I've been making breakfast every Sunday morning for years and will continue to find other ways to make each other happy. I'm beginning to embrace the saying, "Happy wife, happy life."

Day 203 - Grandkids

I don't have any grandkids but I sure hear about them all the time from other retirees. The first question I ask is, "How many do you have?" I see kid's every day where I live and wonder if and when I will be honored with a grandchild of my own. In the meantime, I observe and imagine I'll do fine if I can remember one thing –children are our next generation and although they sometimes ignore their parents and grandparents, it's up to us to be part of their lives.

I haven't been too good at keeping up with my own kids. They are grown, have busy lives and live very far away. If there were more options for living closer, I'm sure I'd move there. We've all made our choices based on need. I never thought I'd live in Florida, or that our kids would live in California, but that's where we are today.

I spoke to each of them today and everything seems fine. We are all where we need to be for now. If and when grandkids arrive, that could change everything. Common sense about retirement tells us that grandkids will keep you young at heart. I'm in no hurry but I sure think they are cute!

Day 204 - Repeats and Do Overs

I've gotten pretty good at making observations and expressing my feelings about retirement. I hope you are entertained by my insights and enjoy my simple point of view.

One of the things I'd like to avoid in retirement is repeats or do-overs, but sometimes it's not possible. The day-to-day, week-to-week and month-to-month of life have begun to blend into each other. I still get the "How's retirement going?" question and want to be able to add a thing or two each time I talk about it. I look forward each day and the repeats or do-overs are about living life on life's terms. I take responsibility and don't mind being accountable, I just need some reminders and encouragement. That's why I'm writing this journal.

Not much has happened this whole week. The weather, my pocketbook and energy levels are all major concerns. I'm resting. Apparently having a simple life is ok by me. Any do overs I've encountered are to be better, faster or more efficient. I like learning and can find a lesson in anything.

Day 205 - You've Come A Long Way

One thing I realized today is that I like to be around retirees. They have come a long way and each one has an interesting story to tell about their lives. You won't be able to tell much by just looking at them either.

Living in Florida has brought me in contact with people from many parts of the country. I've concluded people are different based on where they're from, their education level, job experience, travels and income. Religion, nationality and gender are secondary to understanding people.

We fulfill different roles and have experienced varying amounts of success. Generally speaking, I think a lot of retirees where I live are well-off. Each of them also seems to appreciate where they live compared to where they came from. Many of the ones I've met are kind, considerate and thoughtful and live their retirement with purpose. Not all of them are married, have partners or are in a relationship. That will be another journal entry I'm sure.

I often hear them being asked, "How is it going?" I'm amused when they respond with, "I'm living the dream." The cost of living and weather were top priorities when deciding to retire in Florida. Most of them will tell you that they like where they live and what they are doing now and that what's ahead doesn't yet matter.

Day 206 - Going Far to Get Close

I'm not quite sure why I want to go to the Caribbean when I live in Florida but I do. It's endless summer here and the subtropical weather isn't much different further south. My best guess is there are different people, places and things to see and the grass could be greener somewhere else.

So many people in Florida are from elsewhere and have come to appreciate what I call the Disney effect. You'll see it in restaurants, bars, resorts and any vacation destination in the area. Simply put, it's when someone creates an ideal environment with both exterior and interior designs intended to transport you to some other place or time.

Retirees particularly like to travel to see and do things that have been recommended by others. There's a biking group in town that travels by car for forty minutes to bike in a unique simulated natural setting which includes manufactured hills not common in Florida. I prefer a more honest experience whether it's food, music, art, sports, theatre or anything uniquely local. For example, I think Reggae music sounds better in the Caribbean than in Florida.

Those who view retirement as a permanent vacation may behave with heightened vitality when they travel, even when they never leave the resort where they are staying. I'm much more interested in venturing out from the city center, the resort, or the port to meet the locals and get a true sense of the area I visit. That's my idea of travel. Sometimes you have to go far to get close.

Day 207 - Retirement Blues

It may not seem fair that being retired doesn't make you immune from getting the blues. I'm not directing my attention to depression, that's not my area of interest although I know it exists.

Some recent encounters have made me aware that all is not good or guaranteed when you retire. The expectation of life can have its ups and downs based on the daily actions you take. When I'm feeling down, I focus on making myself available to those in need. Oftentimes, taking the focus away from myself helps to get rid of the blues.

I think keeping busy is also necessary for us to feel fulfilled. I'm not one to want to share in misery or pain and don't appreciate those who do. Stay away from them. Most retirees I've spoken with are private individuals who with time become less able to live through life's obstacles without help. If you lose the sense of hope the blues can come rushing in. An acquaintance once told me he felt that way until he got involved with meals on wheels. Bringing food to those in need opened his eyes to other retirees and he liked making new friends. His age alone helped others appreciate his hard and dedicated work.

Another friend of mine made himself available to someone very sick whose family was not nearby. Each time I see and hear about these kinds of situations I acknowledge the act of kindness and see it as a blessing as well as a cure for the retirement blues. The cross we bear can be lightened with thoughtfulness. Sharing yourself is good in retirement.

Day 208 - Reconnecting

I watched a movie last night about a father and son reconnecting. I've thought about what drew them apart in the first place but I guess that doesn't really matter. I've tried reconnecting with old friends during retirement. My first thought was whether or not they were also retired. If you could explain how and why things changed you may be better able to connect. It's also up to the other person to be receptive.

You may also have an incomplete perspective of all that has been going on with the other person. Don't be quick to judge and give credence to the other side of the story. Retirement is a good time to have a reunion with classmates, friends, business associates and anyone with whom you once shared an experience.

There was a common bond at some time in the past and now may be a good time to reestablish that connection. It was once important to me, and whatever it was that caused the separation shouldn't really matter now.

When you get in touch with the person you are trying to reconnect with, be sure to tell them your reason for reaching out early in the conversation. I always remember my grandparents sitting around at family gatherings and everyone coming to them asking how they were. Their response typically was to brush off the question and turn the attention to how the person asking was doing?

I now know more than ever that I wish I would have asked more questions about old age and their retirement. My grandmother lived to be one hundred and five. She didn't say much past ninety-nine. Staying in touch is important to me. I'm still learning how to do it. There's not a single person who's gone that I don't miss. Who can I reconnect with next?

Day 209 - Let's Get Loud

My wife tells me I often speak too loudly. I'm never aware of it and I don't think I have a hearing problem. I've told her maybe others have a listening problem so I speak up. Retirees need to be heard. We have a lot to say about almost anything. As a group, we represent a large voting segment that are aware of politics and a high percentage of us cast our votes.

I have never forgotten or thought about not voting. I want to be heard now more than ever before. I'll admit my voice goes up in volume when I'm excited. I also know I may not be as funny as I think I am and not all of my life experiences need to be shared. I will however not be silent when it comes to things I'm familiar or have experience with.

I went to a yoga class today that had soft mood music, soft spoken instructors and was warned to keep my voice down to a whisper. I was told in fact by my wife to not speak at all during class. I know there's a time and place for everything so I respected the request. I want everyone to know that retirees need to express themselves and they have a strong life force. So many times in the past, when I saw seniors or anyone older, I didn't think they had much to say. I was wrong about that and many other things.

Day 210 - How Important Is the Bucket List?

A very nice couple I know told me they are going on a National Parks tour. I've been to see many of them but not this particular group. They have seen them before but only in passing and said they promised each other to return in retirement as it was on their bucket list. They were particularly anxious to do it sooner than later because one of the spouse's brothers died before he did anything on his bucket list.

Retirees can and do fulfill many things without stating them as bucket list items. I'm not sure who came up with the idea of a bucket list and assume it must also include an order of importance. I don't have such a list and can't say I really want to even think about making one.

I can probably tell you some things I don't want to do in retirement just as easily as things I'd like to do.

While watching TV last night I saw a movie about the well-known Chelsea Garden Show and Competition and the important designers involved. I'm a big-time fan of gardening and have known about the show for years. After the bucket list discussion, I said I wanted to go to England and see the show soon. I also wondered that if I did make a list how I would decide on what and which order to do things. I would have too many things on my list.

I guess the bucket list is an option for retirees and writing things down doesn't seem like a bad idea. I think if it's important enough to write down then maybe it's important enough to actually do.

Day 211 - Going Along

Am I going along in retirement each day with a happy-go-lucky attitude? Do I burden myself with asking what I should be doing today? It's been three weeks since we came back from vacation yet we haven't ventured to the ocean, seen the beach or gone to our local pool.

The weather has been rainy but Florida still offers many options to go to these places. I haven't given this any thought until right now. I'm beginning to feel stressed about wanting to do more. I look at Facebook every day and become aware of what others are doing. We do have three trips planned before the end of the year and also our daughter's wedding at the end of December. I'm not anxious to spend any more time or money right now so I'll not worry too much.

About the only thing that could get me to go along with someone else's plan would be a unique opportunity to do something that I've never experienced. I don't mind postponing, delaying or even forgetting my own priorities if it serves a higher purpose. I also take my wife's advice very seriously and if she wanted to do something, I would consider it. I guess I'm settling into a retirement mode in which I'm going along without too much trepidation.

Day 212 - Prized Possessions, Forgotten Treasures

If you ask a group of retirees what are their prized possessions, you'll get a wide range of answers. I asked this question recently and some responses included: my wedding ring, motorcycle, house, pocket watch from my grandfather's father, antique cupboard and many more. They can be everyday items or forgotten treasures that relate to a specific individual.

Do you know what your children would say to "What's the one thing that belongs to us that you would want after we're gone?" Some retirees tell me they are saving things for their kids or grandkids. Most retirees have things that their children don't care to have. I went to some consignment shops and saw so many things that were once an important part of someone's life, but now are being offered for sale.

It's best to downsize while you can still decide what you want to do with your worldly possessions. The problem I have is that it's hard to get rid of things you've had for a long time. I say, "If I had them this long, they must be important." On a recent visit to an art museum, I saw many beautiful artworks which were donated and the donors name and date of gifting were on the identification labels. Maybe I'll identify some items that I can donate to an institution or business that can benefit from them. It's best to make these types of decisions sooner rather than later.

Day 213 - Frame of Mind

It seems that retirees are not only different from non-retirees but they are different from other retirees based on the length of time they have been retired. Although they all make life decisions based on cost, need, length of use and importance or necessity, those who have been retired longer, tend to think more about more immediate desires and needs.

Some retirees' decisions surprise me. The one that tops the list is the 84-year-old man who spent $30,000 on four teeth implants. I've also encountered retirees that want to go to or back to college to earn a degree, or get married for the third or fourth time.

I'm thinking about taking some courses to become a master gardener. I already know more about plants than anyone I know. I have forty years' experience and have good results with plants. So why do I need to get certified? I'm not really an expert and we can always learn more. The simple reason is I want to know what I don't know.

Being knowledgeable in retirement can't hurt and it often leads to other areas of interest. Many retirees take classes, lessons and seminars for every imaginable endeavor. I think they do it basically for fun and to become more competent in the activity. Expanding and challenging the mind helps to improve your body and spirit. What's your frame of mind?

Day 214 - Ready, Set, Go!

Retirees like to research everything from restaurants, autos, cruise ships, vacation options and anything that involves time and money. The Internet is great for this but the best advice comes from others' personal experiences and word of mouth.

After deciding on what you can afford, it's easy to justify your actions with the ever-popular phrase, "Well, we're not getting any younger." When choosing an activity, a place to eat or where you take your next vacation, be sure to make the best decision for you.

When I make decisions in retirement, I take a "Ready, Set, Go" approach. By preparing appropriately, I don't need to focus too much on the outcome, but I am still cautious. I am a preservationist and practice moderation. I know my limits. I still get excited when I do new things, and really enjoy this time in my life, I have to remember that, although you go places in retirement, it isn't a race.

Day 215 - Days Daze

It's Friday, right? No, it's Saturday. Friday this week felt like Saturday. Forgetting what day of the week it is happens when you are home sick, in the hospital, on vacation and often when you are retired. Losing track of time may seem like a fortunate state of mind and you think you are living the good life. It's happened to me and each time I laugh it off. It's a retirement state of mind.

This morning I decided it's not funny that you lose interest in what is going on around you and slip into a "Who cares" or "What's the difference" attitude. I want retirement to be an important part of life, not just the end of life. You can live in a daze and not worry about anything or find a purpose in life and continue to seek meaning in each day.

Day 216 - Anniversary

This retirement of mine has all the same birthdays and anniversaries as before. I think each one is more special because I now appreciate things more. It didn't take long in retirement to see this happen.

My wife and I have been together for forty-three years. Many folks I know have passed away and I miss them. Time marches on, sometimes very quickly. I think it's never too late to improve your relationships. The distance between each of us and our loved ones can change.

Our birthday and anniversary celebrations are a good time to restart, reexamine and renew our commitment to what's important and how we share our lives with others. I've become more aware of the fact that we don't know if there will be another day to celebrate.

I get these ideas to change my attitude and make improvements but routines and bad habits distract me from doing what is necessary to change. I'm making new habits and routines to enhance retirement and don't want to create regrets. I don't have to take my wife to Paris, but if she were to say it would be nice, it's probably better to celebrate now.

Day 217 - Kind Words

I've noticed I am more likely to say some kind words to just about anybody during my retirement. I appear to be a softer, kinder man. I'm not the sentimental type but retirement has changed my impression of myself and others.

Compassion has started to finally sink in and the world's a better place because of it. Kind words sound nice and everyone seems to enjoy them. If you are sincere and not manipulative, kindness is a great way to open a conversation. You may even be looked upon with more respect and gain insights from who you are engaging.

I'd offer some considerations to those who don't know what it's like to be retired. Retirees have a carefree attitude. They have fewer time restraints and their schedules are often more flexible. Those who are retired need to remember the pace of life for those who are working and raising a family.

Why not offer a kind word and set an example for others? I sometimes can't believe the compliments that come out of my mouth. I am going to continue to be nicer than I have ever been in the past.

Day 218 - Ladies and Gentlemen

Do men and women retire differently? My entire life I've noticed there is a difference between men and women and now in retirement, it's also true. From my experience I've concluded women think they are going to be retired longer than their spouse and they are more interested in doing more things in retirement.

They are about even in being cautious about spending too much money and like to budget at the same rate. I greatly enjoy speaking with retired women and learn much more about retirement from them than from their spouses. They are particularly more organized and prepared, have insights and pursue the healthy body, mind, and spirit I so desire to incorporate into my retirement.

Many of them want to stay fit, participate with zest in all activities and even dress with much more consideration. Since retirement is an adjustment to new circumstances they also adapt more easily.

I like living in Florida and have wondered if I died what and where would my wife go? She enjoys it here for many of the same reasons but I bet she'd go live closer to our grown-up kids. I've asked other retirees what they would do if they lost their spouse and most don't want to think about it or answer the question.

Retired couples are definitely not the same as single retirees. When changes occur, family and friends may take on a different role. It's, "Love the one you're with, if you can't be with the one you love." That sounds backwards but it still works.

Day 219 - Best Intention

Here I am, living in the moment, day to day, week to week, reflecting and sharing all aspects of retirement. Sometimes I think I am paranoid and overly cautious. But I'm working on that. I prefer to live a healthy life.

In the past, I was preoccupied with some wild expectations, anger and depression, for what now seems like nonsense. I lost sight of what I was really doing to myself and those around me. My selfish and self-serving ways got me in trouble. Even though it was never an intention, my behavior was often immature and it took me a long time to grow up.

Today I live with a more positive outlook and grateful attitude which have been shaped by a reality check. Both good and bad things can make you change. Most retires are having fun and enjoying their time in retirement. Unfortunately, death, suicide, illness, accidents and prior decisions affect us even more in retirement.

I question my intentions often, which may be due to my past behaviors. We certainly do affect one another more than I imagined. We seldom get to choose our next trauma but we can think about how we will react and can be prepared. I'm not interested in writing my memoir because my retirement is all about living in the now.

Day 220 - Bystanders

I have chosen to be a bystander many times. In retirement, I've chosen to be a bystander at first, to learn from observation and more easily decide how I want to fit in.

There's always a group dynamic to contend with and it takes time for it to reveal itself. Some may argue you learn more by doing. I've had to teach myself to listen to learn and learn to listen. I don't expect to always remain a bystander even though I am the shy type and unimposing. I don't handle criticism very well and work well by myself.

At a recent family gathering we decided to play some football and the teams were chosen by a captain. I was a bystander but was needed to fill a team. They picked me last and I wondered why? Was it my age, condition, experience, know-how, lack of enthusiasm? The main focus was to have all the young children playing together. I understood that, but how would they score a winning touchdown without me? I certainly could not accomplish that as a bystander.

Day 221 - More of the Same

Retirement is a game changer for those of us who keep up a busy day-to-day lifestyle. When I was working, I didn't have much time to pursue many hobbies but I managed to enjoy a few and looked forward to any opportunities to have fun.

I think my retirement is just not more of the same because I try new things and have a lot of time to enjoy life. For some time, I thought why not continue doing what you do best? How many hobbies can you have and what's too many? I'm into the balance of mind, body, and spirit and don't want to stray. This is the basis of a successful retirement according to my experiences.

Most of my friends, neighbors and family members know I'm retired and may ask what's he up to or what's he doing now? I hope I never answer with, "More of the same." I have several projects, activities, adventures, travels and would love to share them with anyone who has the time and desire.

I may appear to be a big talker who says a lot of things in regards to what I'm going to do. In the future, I'd like to write a novel, do a short comedy routine and go to England. These aren't more of the same, so wish me luck.

Day 222 - Lucky Numbers

Retirement happens at many different ages, situations and may be welcomed, forced and feared. Today is day 222, not necessarily a lucky number but for this 64-year-old happy to be retired guy, it's a welcomed event. I've benefited from many +55 perks even though the government doesn't consider me to be fully retired until age 66.

I was born on the 11th day of the month. During my 20th business anniversary year I wasn't celebrating much until I entered a contest in which the sponsor who was commemorating his 50th year in business with a special all-expenses paid trip --a Grand Tour of Spain, called to say I had won.

Not only did I immediately have a change of attitude but after the trip my business improved greatly. Many people enter contests and play the lottery. Retirees like to play the lottery and I always enjoy hearing how they plan to spend the money if they win.

I believe in luck. It's a word, so it must exist. Many retirees who worked hard and planned their retirement were lucky to find themselves in a good place without too many worries. We all say good luck to each other and I think it's bad luck not to say "good luck." I've been told I'm a lucky guy and things will work out.

I'll never forget the first time I went to Vegas and watched a man walk up to a roulette table and put a one-hundred-dollar chip on seventeen red. He won and the crowd went nuts with cheers and astonished looks. The woman he was with asked out loud why he picked seventeen. He said it was his lucky number and she was now his lucky girl. I was even more amazed when he gave the roulette spinner a $100 tip.

Day 223 - Kayaking Without a Map

I like talking about retirement to everybody. Even those not retired have an opinion and freely discuss what they know. I went kayaking with a group of retirees and we discussed our impression of the trip, specific sights, encounters with wildlife and an overall critique of our guide who didn't use a map.

I made a big fuss about not having a map and everyone knew I didn't have much experience but never-the-less had an opinion. Being familiar with the area helps but I think a map would give me a sense of security. I don't mind the discovery aspect and I'm becoming more dependent on my instincts because I've gone both ways and see the value of each.

My kayaking experience consists of four trips in which three times I used a map. Not all guides or maps are the same. Highly detailed maps and simple maps function to provide what's important to the user. I learned and observed more because of the guide. If and when I return to any of the sights, I'll have a map or GPS the trip with a phone. Retirement doesn't come with a map but there are guides. You won't get lost or waste time. You'll learn something from them that may expand the experience.

Day 224 - The Error of Your Ways

You are going to do some things that are not to your advantage in retirement. It's not a right and wrong decision but we are humans who have character defects and wanting things to go smoothly only happens with experience. Retirees like to keep themselves comfortable and remain happy. I would say when you are in error, made mistakes, fail or screw up, admit it and seek some guidance with a humble attitude.

You should be old enough to know better but you are learning like everyone else. I've met some retirees who are very socially conscious and go out of their way to make everything right. It's a pleasure to be on the receiving end. It also may not be sincere so be aware of their motives.

I've heard boastful explanations and recognize insecurities and fears. When I'm made aware of these traits in myself or others, I don't hesitate to take action and offer some solutions. A joke and a put down may come to mind but consider the source and recipient. I believe character development continues in retirement. Sports has shown me you can make many errors but still win the game.

Day 225 - Philosophy of Retirement

I've turned into a retirement philosopher, self-designated, but experienced through observations. Writing down my many thoughts has made me think about things I've never expressed. Right or wrong is replaced with better or best to suit my retirement needs.

I've developed a philosophy in which you can ask me any question about my experience and I'll give you my thoughts. Often, I wonder if I should ask others more questions about retirement and see if I missed anything?

I'm sure I have, and will continue to make observations for the entire first year, and maybe beyond. I haven't explored how retirees feel in other countries and that might offer more insight. Cultural differences, belief systems and opportunities will determine your actions or nonactions. In most cases, retirement will do you a lot of good.

It's not too often that we are called upon to verbalize our philosophy of retirement. I encourage everyone to examine, state or write down some of your thoughts just to see what comes of it. Private time for reflection can be an activity in retirement. I wouldn't want to miss out on discovering something about myself.

When I'm asked, "How's retirement going?" I usually say "Great." I mean it and quickly give examples of why I think so. My daily reflection sounds like I have doubts or am unhappy but it's more about staying honest. The deep thinker in me says, "Actions speak louder than words." I'm sure you've heard that before. That's my retirement philosophy! Are you happier now in retirement than you were prior?

Day 226 - Father's Day

Today is like so many other days of observation. It's what you make it. Sometimes you're lucky and others offer suggestions for you. Do you put out flags on flag day? Do you labor on Labor Day? You get my point. I'm sometimes disappointed when there aren't any plans. Two of my three kids are out of the country. The third asked what I wanted to do today. The three of them also got me a gag gift which I didn't find funny. I immediately thought well maybe that's what I deserve.

Being a bigger part in their lives in this year of retirement would show them I want to be of service and it's not all about me. This is my first Father's Day in retirement like every other first in retirement so what do I expect?

Do I care enough to wonder? I do and if I'm being a little overly sensitive, welcome to the new me because that's how I feel. I don't like the feeling and it's more than a disappointment. My solution and advice for retirees is, don't let it get you down.

Feeling sorry for yourself, especially without cause, is self-defeating and should last only a short time. If you wallow in your selfishness for too long, it becomes more difficult to take appropriate action.

Being grateful for what you have is better than being disappointed for what you don't. My kids know I don't want any more than some kind words. We always have a good time when we are together. Loving others and being loved makes a difference in retirement. I'll just have to make it a Happy Father's Day myself and invite my son and wife along.

Day 227 - What Condition is Your Condition In?

Am I in the same condition I was when I first retired? Have I gained weight? That knee of mine is sure giving me a lot of concern. How much have I spent in retirement? I have an ongoing interest in asking the same questions and often worry about staying informed and remaining honest in the evaluation. No excuses!

During the early retirement stage, I was most concerned about developing and maintaining the mental, physical, emotional, spiritual and financial aspects of my new life. I have stressed that an honest assessment of each aspect is the most essential way to be successful. I'm hoping my obsession over each detail will help me fulfill my needs.

Am I happy? What good am I doing? The bucket list has me thinking in so many directions, sometimes I lose sight of my priorities in retirement? Do I always have to have something to look forward to see and do?

It's only June and my daughter's wedding in December has us focused mostly on finances and travel plans. We look forward to the celebration and are excited with joy and anticipation each day. We haven't delayed any plans; we've just set our priorities straight.

In case you haven't noticed, I like to offer advice on everything, but you'll have to examine what's right for you.

What's your condition? How are you feeling? I think it's important to ask questions but you must answer these questions for yourself, or someone else will.

Day 228 - Priorities

I'm starting to have a better sense of what's important and most necessary for me in retirement. My routine is based on my energy level and mental capacity. I work in the garden almost every day; weeding, watering and making observations and improvements. I think of the biblical reference "you shall reap what you sow," and I see how it also applies to retirement.

What's missing? Did I forget or neglect anything? I seem to make adjustments according to set priorities, but what's my motivation? Each of us does things for a purpose whether or not we realize what it is. How effective we are at this is probably something only we can decide for ourselves.

The occasional feedback from friends and family on what we're up to and the results or improvements help us recognize the worthwhileness of our actions. Their comments aren't my motivation but I do like encouragement, recognition and an acknowledgement now and then.

I've reorganized my garage at least four times in the last five years. Three of them have taken place in the last six months of retirement. I should do the same with my life. You have to get your ducks in a row to make real progress. If you can do more than one thing at a time, you're a better man than I. I'm going to set some priorities besides the garage, it always gets messy no matter what.

Day 229 - Timeframes and Dates

We purchased a couple of kayaks recently and have gone out only once. There are a lot of places to go boating and we look forward to exploring the area and having more fun. I told my wife each time we're done kayaking and, on our way home, we should discuss and plan our next possible site to explore.

Whether it's a day trip, weekend excursion or weeklong vacation you can divide the event into three parts. First you have the idea and anticipation. Secondly there's the activity itself. Thirdly you reflect on the experience and plan the next excursion you'd like to have in order to continue the fun.

My life and retirement are going by fast. We started out with a calendar and marked out each month. When I looked at the calendar today it was on the previous month and I haven't bothered looking at it or making any additions or changes. I make a big deal in retirement about staying aware and having a routine that is flexible. Losing sight of an idea and letting time pass is not what I planned to do.

I do love the freedom of not having to be totally predictable every day. Retirees can keep a calendar as an easy way to organize themselves. I think you will still feel retired and won't be pressured into what is written down. It's your retirement, so plan on having fun!

Day 230 - Day and Night

Today there are equal hours of daylight and nightlight. A perfect balance of time -- both 50/50 and 12/12. I don't often wonder how to spend my evenings in retirement. I have considered the fact that by age sixty the average time spent sleeping is twenty years of your life. Spending an entire third of your life sleeping, seems like a lot, but it is a necessity.

The other eighteen hours are part of the day and night. I go to bed between 10 PM and 11 PM and try to rise at 7 AM each morning. Weekends are no different. Each evening there are two things that always seem to happen -- dinner and watching TV. The amount of time spent on each is something to consider.

I've gone out like other retirees in the evenings to enjoy a movie, visit friends, share a meal at a restaurant, enjoy a concert, etc. I'll be honest, I don't like driving at night, staying out late or being tired the next day. I like to wind down, relax and prefer to sit still later in the evening.

My wife makes a lot of phone calls and is more proactive in sharing her experiences and asking about others. I recognize the value and need to work on this. Going on the computer may occasionally be an option but I rarely need to because I've done it earlier or it can wait until tomorrow. Maybe I can find a nighttime activity like poker night with the guys. I could go to more meetings, which are most often in the evenings. I've been an active participant for over sixteen years and going to meetings has replaced going out to bars.

Turning off the TV, finding a book or magazine, making phone calls are all options. I bet if I give it some more thought, my nights could be as meaningful as my days. I know they won't often be equal.

Day 231 - Congratulations

I sold my business five years ago and decided to congratulate the young man who purchased it. I'll give him a call. During his first year in business he called often and I enjoyed our talks. I haven't heard from him for about two years and assume he is doing fine. My business was thirty years old and had many wonderful loyal customers. I once told him if things don't go well it will be his fault, but now I want to know how well he and his family are doing.

I try not to forget to acknowledge birthdays, anniversaries, graduations or anything that is an accomplishment. I still remember how many people congratulated me on my retirement. I was deeply touched that they acknowledged the accomplishment. Recognition is important for everyone.

When asked to play an original tune in music class I got what I considered to be my first applause. I hadn't been playing very long when this happened and didn't really expect more than a few words of encouragement. Looking back on the experience I loved the surprise and know now why it could be addicting.

After retirement there may not be too many more congratulations but I look forward to weddings and grandchildren. Most of the retirees I've spoken with say they have earned their retirement. It came about with effort and planning. In some cases, sacrifices were made and these retirees have gained my respect and I'll tell them to be proud of themselves. Life throws us many challenges, opportunities and decisions that need to be made. A word of acknowledgement for a job well done is cause for celebration. Retirees love to party!

Day 232 - Obstacles

Retirement will give you time but not necessarily patience, tolerance or acceptance. I've become set in my ways in terms of beliefs and actions. I've heard this about older folks when I was younger and recall my grandmother saying it about my grandfather.

When something interrupts me, I seem to immediately get upset and act disturbed. The creed of "leave me alone, I'm retired" has hit me. I have the attitude of let the next fellow deal with this or that. Retirees should be on the lookout for delays, disappointments and distress.

These things just happen so what's the fuss? I guess having dealt with it before doesn't make it easier. Rather I become less patient and say "enough already." I'm glad when it's over but now I have to deal with how I reacted? Was it a normal, healthy way, or was I part of the problem?

I was recently banned for life from eBay and don't know exactly what I did wrong. I think they thought I might be a crook with all the trouble I had getting an account. I avoided telling anyone because I was embarrassed and didn't need their service right away. I finally had to call to find out why I was banned. After two hours of waiting on the phone and speaking with four people I'm good with eBay.

My wife helped me accept the challenge and overcome the obstacles. It's ok to ask for help in retirement as long as you tell the truth and don't act helpless. People recognize obstacles and can help you learn how to avoid or work through them. Be sure to thank them or you may cause another obstacle to happen.

Day 233 - Meet the New Guy

It's going to happen. You'll meet someone who is newly retired. Your experience, outlook, attitude and general well-being can be an example, so help them if they ask for any pointers in their transition. I don't have much experience but I have more than them so that's all that's important.

I was introduced to a stranger and after a casual two-hour conversation we made a connection. I learned how we were similar and how we differed. I was a Midwesterner and he grew up on the East Coast. I was self-employed and he only worked for large corporations. We went back and forth with excitement and wonder. In retirement you can compare and contrast all you want until you get to what's important. The differences explain a lot but not everything.

Some retirees go through a metamorphosis and reinvent themselves. Their new freedom now is an exploration of themselves, which many do for the first time in their lives. I have more patience with the new guy and enjoy sharing my thoughts and anticipating the response. I want him to feel welcomed and offer a handshake, a smile and ensure him that retirement is a good thing. So, join the club!

Day 234 - Wheeler Dealer

I don't think I have ever been such a wheeler dealer as I have since I've retired. I'm not without previous experience in making deals but my recent obsession has me always asking for more. Is my motive to save money? What makes me think I need more?

What gives me the audacity to expect that retirement owes me something? With this kind of attitude, you risk creating anger, resentment and even some foul play. I wouldn't intentionally piss off a repairman, waitress, clerk or merchant. But I've come to realize that I've been using my retirement status and age to my advantage a little too often.

I've also seen other retirees exhibit mistrust and place unnecessary demands on others. I once asked an instigator of poor behavior if they felt as if the way they acted was ok and their response was, "I'll never see them again."

Being retired doesn't give you a license to be a jerk and if you are, you better find out why. I know retirees often get taken advantage of and may not represent themselves very well. People don't always respect you just because you are older, alone or retired. I wouldn't suggest you act dumb, ignorant or needy either.

Try to act with respect and show confidence in retirement. You may be tempted to use any and all tactics to take advantage of the situation. For example, I've heard some retirees, say, "I'm on social security or I'm on a fixed income and I can't afford it," when I know they can. You aren't fooling anyone, except yourself.

The most successful wheeler dealers have actually figured out that the best way to get what they want is to be nice, not demanding. Be patient, rather than yell out and cause a scene. I think retirees will get more if they say less. The most successful wheeler dealers realize that if they are kind, good things will naturally come to them.

Day 235 - Road Trips

Two recent road trips, short ones returning home the same day, have given me an appreciation for where I live. There is a lot to see and do in Florida! One concern about our trips has been that we don't seem to do much on the second day because we packed in too many activities the day before.

Retirees like nice weather and Florida has endless summer which happens to be the state motto. I lived in Iowa for thirty years prior to moving here and can only recall a handful of road trips. Nothing against Iowa, it's a lovely state and I'm forever grateful for raising our family and running my business there. We just didn't give it the time.

With my retirement status I have a big desire to be an explorer and as long as I am able, I will look forward to continuing to get out and about. In the past I had excuses, which looking back, I wish I didn't make. I think every state in the US has so much to offer.

I can't believe all the festivals I've read about. "If you've been to one, you've been to them all," is not the least bit true. Some retirees I've spoken with may not share my enthusiasm for fairs and festivals. I'd like to go to a festival each week, travel across America and be gone for months. I think about the variety of food, music, and cultures, and the uniquely regional festivals. In Iowa, I wouldn't want to miss the Sweet Corn Festival. In Florida there's an orange festival, strawberry festival and my favorite -- the seafood festival .

Each of these road trips includes free people watching, which I enjoy. I do wonder how is it that when I pack the car for one of these road trips, I always seem to come home with more than I packed.

Day 236 - Arguing with Fate

Retirement is my sole preoccupation and my real job, as I like to tell everyone, is working to stay healthy. It didn't take long before I realized you can try all you like, there's just going to be trouble and some unexplainable problems. I'm not the type to ask why this is happening to me now.

As I continue in retirement, I've seen and heard about others fate through conversations, readings, movies, books and just observing. I've seen and read a lot more about it as a student of retirement which has allowed me to make some conclusions.

So often I wonder why people like to argue with fate? When you are older you may not have many options. I get paranoid when I think of the day that I may not be able to continue playing pickleball? I enjoy it so much that I wish I did it earlier in life and now I want to do it more often.

I see widows and widowers and can't image myself alone. I know all kinds of things are going to happen whether I like it or not. Now my retirement has me not asking, "What are you going to do about it," but rather "What are you able to do about it?"

I believe in luck, both good and bad. I just read about a man who got struck by lightning while walking on the beach. Maybe he shouldn't have been out there but he was and so were others. I've walked the beach many times in my sixty-plus years on earth, he on the other hand was 23-years-old and didn't have a chance to argue with fate.

Day 237 - You Owe It to Yourself

Retirement can make you feel guilty. I have a great respect and admiration for each retiree who has worked hard making a living and continues in retirement to be of service to their community, family and friends. I don't do much in this area right now and want to decide what to try. No one can accuse me of being lazy but I see that I'm more selfish as I age.

I've been told by experienced retirees that you owe it to yourself to give retirement some time and trial and error is going to be part of the learning curve. It takes time to learn how, what, where and why you do what you do.

I once thought that if you feel you owe someone or somcthing your time and experience, it's because you had once been on the receiving end and now want to give back. Showing respect and concern for those who deserve it, may be your motivation to help others.

If you save someone in danger or just harm's way, they may tell you "I owe you my life." That's about as serious as it can get. Even the little things we do for others can have a huge impact on their lives. We can't solve all the world's problems but we can make some people's struggles easier to bear with our help.

What do we owe ourselves in retirement? Time to help others? Time to explore new places and try new things? My suggestion is to take the time you need to decide what you want to dedicate your time to.

Some retirees may want to shut the door to the past and live a new life with less involvement and more introspection. They want to be free of commitments, schedules, and other people's problems. If that door you're shutting has a window I suggest you get a curtain. When someone or something comes calling, see who it is and ask questions before you make any decisions. The most important thing you owe yourself is the truth.

Day 238 - Positive Attitude

I've heard about attitude since before the first grade. I generally don't have a positive attitude. I'm suspect about people, places and things. Mainly I've seen a lot of disappointment and wonder about reliability. Not having a generally positive outlook hasn't made me bitter, resentful or someone you don't want to be around.

I'm cautious with actions and often outspoken with words. I am working on improving this as a life's mission. In retirement it can help to see the good rather than bad in situations. I know that in sports and business it's your attitude that can make you a winner. Success is never guaranteed and you need an attitude adjustment to get yourself headed in the right direction. My mission is to hold off on comments and thoughts until I really know that what I say or do serves the right purpose.

Many retirees have chosen to live in plus fifty-five communities and they share many thoughts and have common interests. Their primary purpose is to be safe, have fun and enjoy an affordable retirement. Their attitude is they are living life as it should be or could be. I didn't choose this approach or lifestyle but I do find it very appealing for those reasons.

I don't want to be around negative, unhappy retirees who seem confused, bitter and living in distress. Older folks have more physical and mental issues and after these are addressed their outlook quickly changes. If you want to enjoy retirement, I suggest you be around others who have a positive attitude. It won't hurt.

Day 239 - Drama

We all make mistakes in retirement. We say and do things that might bite us in the ass, and then the drama begins. I don't consider my retirement very exciting so why not let some drama enter into it?

I like to watch people react and now I am able to be the director, actor and writer of the script to my retirement life. It's about as unreal as it gets. It may bring attention to yourself, but what's wrong with that? You want the plain and simple truth? Avoid it and you'll sleep better at night and have less to worry about.

The childlike and immature are often found in older retired adults. If your retirement is idle it may bring out the worst in you. Being on stage or sitting in the audience are not the only two options. You should consider the role of the usher in retirement. You're there to help people find their place and you can then enjoy watching the professionals do their jobs – lighting, makeup, the director and the actors. It doesn't cost you to see the show either.

After the show you'll offer more assistance but if you're lucky you may get invited to the after party where the real drama begins. You have many roles to fulfill in retirement. Go for the gusto, but avoid the drama.

Day 240 - Quietude

I get asked if I'm retired so often that I now respond with how many months I have been retired. It's an unbelievable eight months already! I've been asked if I am used to being jobless or not having a boss or not having to go to work each day. My next response is I still have a job and it's staying healthy. I've also added that I've taken up studying quietude. It always gets a laugh and leads to an explanation.

Being still and staying quite is not easy. In retirement you have to practice with prayer and meditation to stay calm and experience serenity. I didn't know I wasn't calm until I began to feel different in retirement. I sensed becoming more emotional and sensitive. I feel more appreciative and show gratitude with more ease. I am more in touch with these emotions and I'm willing to explore an inward examination of who I am. I observe and wonder about things with purpose and truly find joy in simple experiences.

I can sit on the beach and watch the waves coming in, people walking by and birds flying above, all at the same moment. At night lying in bed and reflecting on the day soon leads to peaceful sleep. My mornings begin with coffee time with my wife and I'll water my plants and listen to the cardinal's song coming from the nearest tree. There is a particular bird who won't give up his loud and long song. I'm not sure if he is a player doing an audition or just hasn't found a mate because no one is interested. His song is remarkable! I've never heard such variety and experienced such enthusiasm.

I saw cardinals in Iowa often but rarely stopped to listen very long. Seeing these birds in Florida did surprise me and I investigated to see if they were native. My quietude lately has slipped away but it was worth it just to admire the wonderful sound. Being retired is changing me. The interruption of the quite morning is now an anticipation of whether or not he will come back to that tree? I'll have to be quite and wait and see.

Day 241 - Rainy Season

I just realized that this is my first summer being retired. In Florida that means the rainy season and time spent inside. I'd like to avoid this and if I had the opportunity I'd go on a trip or plan to visit friends or family up North. Many of them would like to visit us in the winter months so that could be worked out. Now could be the time to make plans and offer myself other alternatives during this time of year.

The rainy season whether it's here or up North does alter your mood and my retired status should make me more tolerant, but it doesn't. In Iowa, we would hibernate for months because of the cold. This rainy time of year with short bursts of rain each day has me wanting an immediate solution.

I don't argue with Mother Nature and is there anywhere on earth that is perfect? I'm singing a new song. Instead of, "Rain, rain go away," how about, "Rain, rain I'm on my way to find a sunny day in a place not far away." Retirement has brought out the poet in me, making me more expressive.

Day 242 - What Have You Overlooked

Sometimes in retirement you may start out with a good intention or direction but soon begin to overlook the obvious. You can also become slack, uninterested, distracted and even uncaring.

This is the time to ask yourself, why you did it in the first place? What's most important about the activity? Does anyone really care if you continue to do this or not?

This behavior can be a sign that you are not focusing on your retirement as a matter of choice but feeling you can waste away time and money and it's yours to do. I call this a bad attitude and misguided life.

Not caring about your retirement leads to problems that will affect your mental, physical and emotional needs. Your spiritual side might be buried in a cave and unable to come out.

The many facets of a human being need to be expressed and free to expand. The big boulder that's keeping you inside yourself was placed there by you. You prefer being in the sunshine and staying happy through involvement but every day you walk by this boulder and soon don't notice it.

There are people who will help you and you just have to ask. If you wonder if you may have overlooked some things in retirement you probably have. I want to be successful in retirement and stay happy. I think it's a journey that I am preparing myself for. I've been in the cave and found protection and comfort.

If you give yourself the opportunity to look around, something will grab your attention and draw you out. There are many sides of life that should not be overlooked. Stay involved and remember, it's okay to retreat every once in a while, for comfort and security. Just don't retreat for too long.

Day 243 - Alone and Unafraid

I've noticed I'm accountable to my spouse who recently retired but I haven't made myself accountable for her. There are many retirees who are single or alone due to divorce or death, and they make the best of their situation. Not having this experience doesn't stop me from having some thoughts or opinions. In the past, I would offer advice even when not asked.

I believe if you fall off a horse you should get back on the saddle and try again. The view is better from up there and you will get to where you want to go much faster. Fear rules so many of our lives. I ask myself how does someone overcome anything. I wonder am I braver with my wife or because of my wife? Some of us lead by example and others follow along. We should offer special treatment to widows, widowers, divorcees and any fearful retirees we meet. How would you want to be treated?

It takes a lot of fortitude and courage to face adversity. I can't pretend to know how alone or lost they feel but know that each person can be made to feel less alone. Being ashamed of your fears is not uncommon and often leads to isolation. If you find yourself alone and afraid, try to share yourself and all that you can offer. I know we're all worth it.

Day 244 - Independence Day

When you're retired one of the best things you can do is become independent. The less you need the more you have. I call it peace of mind. It's not something you can buy. Keeping your needs simple allows you to negotiate your retirement and give it your best shot.

This holiday reminds me of what is important and how we shouldn't take what we have for granted. You can observe and create your own celebrations but keep in mind there needs to be a basis to each of them. Do we know why we have fireworks on the Fourth of July? In fact, why do we have fireworks at all? Most of us like the oohs and aahs when they explode. It's also the last thing we observe on this day. It's the culmination of a fun-filled day.

We should always appreciate our freedom. I think of the fireworks as the manifestation of a powerful and beautiful force under our control. Why not live our lives with a bang?

Day 245 - After the Party

After each weekend or holiday party, I feel refreshed about retirement. The first thing I do is a general cleanup, which I do in parts, not to be overwhelmed. Next, I savor the event by reflecting on what did or did not happen. What did I like?

Retirement in this situation is great because you don't have to go to work the next day. Yesterday's Fourth of July party was a blast and six hours of food, drink and conversation flew by. I helped whenever I could and everyone seemed happy. We observe, celebrate and appreciate this holiday for reminding us of all we have to be grateful for. The next occasion may not be for months. What can I do in the meantime to continue the good feelings?

Every day in retirement can't be a party, can it? No, because I don't have the energy. All the preparations and cleanup aren't bad if you have some help. Today I'll probably concentrate on getting much needed rest and have a quiet day. I never considered an after-party plan. I once went to a wedding that had an after party that was both a surprise and indication of how special the bride and groom regarded their guests. That's one wedding I'll never forget.

Maybe after my experience I'll come up with an after-party idea for retirees. It might not make us feel younger but we'll have something to talk about.

Day 246 - Now

I retired when I thought it made sense. A financial advisor and others would probably disagree. Any time before the suggested age of sixty-six that I could quit working made sense to me. When I said now's the time to retire, I didn't realize how or what that would involve. Now that I do, I can honestly say that the cycle of day and night are much more enjoyable. Less worry and stress are the first benefits but you do have to do something.

I had to try and do different things at different times to appreciate the outcome. I actually made some rules for myself and followed them. My daily routine hasn't changed nor has adding and subtracting activities. I have, however, begun to live in the now more often.

Because I'm more flexible, I'll bend some rules or make concessions for opportunities. I typically plan ahead and will consider a Plan B but rarely go to Plan C or D. Living retirement in the now took some time to experience and I appreciate having tried it. I'm a student of life and it sure makes sense to worry less and enjoy more. It's now time to know the importance of living in the now.

Day 247 - Who Ate My Ribs?

People in retirement become more possessive of their time, money and energy. I certainly worked hard for what I have and can't start over. What you have is what you get. My next-door neighbor was kind enough to bring me a sampling of smoked ribs. I mentioned it to my son and for some reason he decided to eat them all. He said he thought I had already had some and the one's left over were for him to try. Not the case and I thought of them as all mine, given to me and not offered as such.

Maybe after a thorough investigation of circumstances and review of my emotions I would be better able to make an assessment. Retirees like me don't want to miss out on a special treat. Maybe I was taken advantage of. Did I do all I could to protect the gift I received?

After a nebulous explanation there was only one conclusion. I am responsible for everything in retirement. If something happens or doesn't happen, I'm not the victim but rather the enabler. I guess I'll continue to live and learn. Sharing is not something I'm opposed to but I'm just selective when it comes to certain things.

Day 248 - Overdo It

I went kayaking today and overdid it. It's not something I was prepared to deal with. My back didn't get sore but when I tried to move or bend, I could feel the discomfort. I've told myself in retirement I should take things at a slower pace. There's never a reason to rush or overdo it. These simple rules need to be followed.

Managing your limits changes with age. I thought I was in good shape but this workout has me paying the price of over estimating by capacity. Anyone's limits in retirement are only revealed after the experience. My youthful attitude doesn't help and knowing what to do next time is now my biggest lesson.

When we get visitors here in Florida, I always stress drink more water, wear sunscreen and don't forget your sunglasses. Experience has taught me more than someone's advice. I like to learn the hard way and need to learn my own lesson.

Retirement has taught me when something happens you can start by asking why but it's more important to spend your time answering, "What am I going to do about it?" The "I wouldn't be in this situation if," statement doesn't matter as much. It's water under the bridge syndrome. I really should know better but I'm only human.

Day 249 - Perspective

I know my surroundings very well. I see the same things every day but they don't always appear the same or familiar. Before I retired, I never gave much thought to where I would end up. After I decided to retire, my main concerns were affordability and weather. Snow was not to be included.

Now that I am retired in Florida, I probably spend more time landscaping than doing anything else. I consider a process of fine tuning, improving, changing and adjusting the perspective. I even added solar lights to enhance the look at night.

When I was a youngster riding my bike through the neighborhood, I observed a lot of older folks tending to their yards. Many of them were pulling weeds, bent over, some with gloves and they never seemed to be able to stand straight up. I thought this was what people who had nothing better to do did. It didn't look like fun.

When they were done it appeared to be an improvement and looked nice, but why didn't more people do it? I'd call it a lot of work and I guessed some people just didn't care about these things.

I'm now one of the folks who does this stuff and I actually like it. Enhancing my surroundings in retirement gives me a pride of ownership and I enjoy the colors, textures, growth and development of the landscape to the point where I call it a hobby. My entire neighborhood more or less looks like this which is one reason we like it so much. I wonder how an urban dweller would react to so much manicuring and care.

I consider the time I spend landscaping as having a relationship with nature. I don't like weeds and it's a weekly year-round job to maintain a Florida landscape. Behind my house is the jungle and it reminds me of the natural environment. Observing the life cycle is why I do it and my perspective is always changing. I may not have the four seasons but I do have an endless summer.

Day 250 - Goddess and Ghost

I like being retired and observing what goes on in the neighborhood. I'm not a busy body, more a student of life. I can come and go at different hours throughout the day and see a variety of kids going to school, adults going off to work and retirees out and about.

I live in a large park-like development and see many regulars walking their dogs, jogging, and doing yard work or outside chores. The two I see often and look forward to are, by my description, the goddess and the ghost.

The goddess has beautiful bronze skin and is very fit. She walks and runs throughout the community and everyone I've spoken to knows who I am talking about. The ghost has very white, almost translucent skin and white hair. She wears high heels, carries an umbrella to shade herself from the sun and only walks the same path from her home to the front gate and back each day.

In my estimation, both of these characters are older than sixty. They have nice outfits and I think of them as a personification of one person in different stages of life. Retired guys like me have an imagination and after I get an acknowledgment by them from a brief sidewalk passing, I wonder how they perceive me and my enthusiast greeting.

Unlike the goddess and the ghost, not too many adults pay much attention to retirees like me. We tend to blend together in Florida and are expected to be polite but that's about it. These two, however, stand out and I appreciate them for it.

When I mention an encounter with either the goddess or the ghost to others, I usually get a funny look. Many retirees work at looking good. Some excel and work hard at it. These two ladies inspire me and I like to witness their acknowledgement to passersby. I spend as much time outside as I can because you never know what you're missing unless you're there.

Day 251 - Look Both Ways

On my every-so-often bike ride I watched as a fellow rider, my wife, got hit by a car while she was crossing the street. She was thrown to the ground but not seriously hurt. I had passed the car first, acknowledged the driver through eye contact and crossed but he didn't anticipate another rider and was looking the other way when she passed.

He was definitely of retirement age and quickly responded with concern. I stopped and returned to help and direct any discussion of each side of the story. She was helped up and wanted to continue her ride after exchanging some words with the car driver. She wasn't wearing a helmet but only rode on the sidewalk. I concluded that each of them needed to look both ways and be safer crossing the street. I also thought maybe I was just lucky to have crossed first and wondered whether the driver had his mind on the road or on a discussion he was having with his passenger, who didn't bother getting out of the car after the accident. How strange!

Retirees should play it double safe when it comes to venturing into traffic. We so often hear about accidents involving older drivers. Precaution means prevention. I've had my share of accidents and it always involves shock. You soon recover and go on with life. Watch out and try looking both ways, twice.

Day 252 - What's Wrong with Me?

I think self-improvement has become a theme in my retirement. It started out with asking how can I improve things around here. Then it turned to saying, "Don't I have anything else to worry about in retirement?" You would think taking it easy is good as well as adding a variety of activities, because you have to do something in retirement.

I find purpose in my actions but I am still curious about what keeps people motivated to do the things they do. When I want to make myself or things around me better, how do I get motivated? I know retirement is an Exploratorium and, for me, it's easy to say, "To each his own," when it comes to actions and the way we spent time.

I know of many retirees who do very little each day. I lowered my daily expectations early on in retirement and it has been beneficial because I'm happier. I've spent time and money often enough and not appreciated the outcome. Can you really escape from your past, reinvent yourself? When you're asked what has happened to you do you respond with, "That's what retirement does to you."

That seems dramatic but retirement has meant a lot of changes for me. I always work with what I've been given and make the best of any situation. I consider it one of my strengths. I won't make a fuss unless it's really objectionable. If I can continue to make improvements in retirement it means I care about my retirement and the outcome. My route doesn't have a road map. I don't believe I'm going the wrong way but I might be. Is there really a wrong way? Let's not overanalyze today!

Day 253 - What I Want

I hadn't gone sailing for so long because of weather, that nothing was going to stop me except rain, enough wind and someone to join me today. I was half right in anticipation but the experience was a waste of time. I was mad at myself for being stubborn and letting my desires over take me. This may mark the first time in retirement that I made a decision to try to have a "what the heck" attitude.

I knew from the start the odds were against me but gave credence to the possibility that the weatherman may be wrong. Besides the inconvenience to my wife who joined me, I didn't have a plan B and was grateful she wasn't as disappointed as I was. Retirement makes it easier to act on impulse but being free and easy going doesn't guarantee anything.

I have to learn to better balance my desires with seeing the relative truth in a situation. I've been told this is a sign of maturity. I'm mature in age and may need to remind myself that I might not always get what I want but I can get what I need. In this case a plan B, C or even D would have helped. I guess I should practice what I preach.

Day 254 - A Thrill

I saw that some friends posted fishing pictures on Facebook and immediately thought what a thrill it must have been to catch such a big fish. I've been retired for months and I've not had anywhere near such a thrill and I questioned why not? Would I like to have a thrill and why do I even think I need one? I guess I did recently go jet skiing and that was a thrill. Maybe retirement is not a thrill-seeking time but it can be.

The feeling you get is unique. You're in the moment experiencing a controllable situation which can get out of control. When you're fishing for the big one you have to get out on the water in the right location, have the proper equipment and bait. Your expectation is never a guarantee.

Thrills don't have to be dangerous, they only seem that way. People gamble for the thrill of a possibility. Many folks go on amusement park rides, climb great heights and set out for unseen and unknown places. What other thrills are out there that I don't know of? I've heard of the thrill of the chase. Then there's also the thrill of the moment. We all have a sense of fear and it's uncomfortable to those not accustomed to it. Each thrill we seek depends on this fear factor.

The more experience you have the less the thrill. While I don't have much retirement experience and the thrill of the first few weeks is long gone, I think I do have some thrill seeking in me. In fact, I'm thrilled to be alive. Retirement is a thrill and I just didn't know it!

Day 255 - Thoughtfulness

I've met so many nice, thoughtful people in retirement. They've gone out of their way to help and encourage me and others. I've sensed a general well-wishing among retirees.

"I guess we've made it this far, we don't know how long it will last, so let's enjoy the ride," are just a few of the generalizations I've heard about retirement from other retirees.

Just because we don't know how long retirement will last, doesn't mean we shouldn't still assess the decisions we make. I've had discussions about this with my wife and realistically, I hope I last ten years. If I last longer, thank God! I also mentioned in these discussions that women often spend more years in retirement, often over twenty years.

Whether it's long or short we should try to set examples for ourselves and be more kind, thoughtful and grateful in retirement. It's never too late to make amends or show a different side of yourself. When you think of others, they may open themselves up to you and share a life experience. I go to a 12-step meeting each week and have attended meetings elsewhere for sixteen years.

I go to help others by offering thoughtful comments, sharing my experience and displaying an example of hope and strength in community. I'm not naturally a "think of others" kind of guy. I've witnessed it so much in retirement that I'm more prone to accept it as the way it should be. It's up to me to help others like I've been helped.

Day 256 - Surprises

When you're retired don't be surprised when you do strange things without a reason. I decided to send some gifts to some old friends and also to my only brother. I wanted it to be a surprise because I like surprises. If or when I get asked why I did it I'll probably respond with, "Don't you like surprises?" I honestly don't have any other good reason. I'm not interested in attention and my generosity is modest. I'm more of an instigator who's been accused of spontaneous behavior when I'm most excited.

In this case, I did it to spread goodwill. I suppose I and other retirees do have ulterior motives in some actions. I think my mother had them very often. It was cute now and again but I did see through them.

I've met retirees who act poor or helpless and portray themselves as needy. I've heard the "I'm on social security," line a lot. I hope my gifts say that I thought about you. If you've ever had a pay-it-forward experience you know it's a feel- great moment. You want to surprise others and share in the joy and goodwill. Surprise someone and you may surprise yourself. You'll be glad you did. Surprise!

Day 257 - Critic Without a Cause

Retirees like to receive benefits and enjoy the little extras they receive. In many cases they've earned them through loyalty clubs, long-time memberships and sponsorships. What happens when you're not satisfied or things come up short? You know you deserve better and you need to speak up to get some satisfaction.

Retirement is not the time to roll over, turn the other cheek or let it go. If you have a problem, don't give it to someone else either. When it's time to communicate or comment, make sure you know what you're talking about. Retirees like to compare and contrast. I studied the art of criticism in college and it goes without saying that either you know what you're talking about or you don't. Facts are facts.

Now when I listen to retirees or read reviews, I take on a different perspective. I'm retired so what do I think as a retired person? We all have our opinions just like we all have our excuses. I watched Rebel without a Cause recently and could relate to the angst of not knowing what to do.

I'm more or less content in the day-to-day retirement lifestyle. My egomaniac behavior and inferiority complex are starting to go away. My age and retirement have shifted my focus on what's important and necessary for my wellbeing and happiness. My cause is to live long and be free!

Day 258 - Grand Openings

I went to another grand opening. It's been my third one in less than a year. Things are prospering in Florida in this area at an alarming rate. New homes and neighborhoods bring good and bad changes.

Each of these grand openings began mid-week and continued into the weekend. Each one had more than five hundred people waiting to get in for a first look and prize giveaways. There were many retirees in line when I went mid-week. It was like a happening of the sixties with people gathered to enjoy something new.

The prizes helped but I would have gone anyway. Most retirees do appreciate the giveaways, specials, deals, samples and the ability to brag about being there when it opened. I had so much fun that I went to one twice, two days in a row.

Retirees are on the lookout for new things and question how they will affect their lives. I almost wish I could feel and act the same for every new happening.

I usually don't go to store closings, liquidation sales, auctions or even garage sales. There may be some deals, but I'm not excited about other people's discarded items and leftovers. I once went to all of these in my younger years. I think of retirement as a sort of grand opening at least in the first few months. It's new to us, we look forward to it and experience it with the hope of some good things to come. The prize isn't that we made it but rather that we can share it with others.

Day 259 - Carefree

For some reason people may think that being retired gives you a carefree attitude. You're looked at as fancy-free with no need to care about the day-to-day struggles going on in life.

How often have you ever said you don't have a care in the world? Retirees may act this way but about the only thing I'm careless about is getting to work on time. That's because I don't have a job to go to.

I like being free spirited and don't miss the eight to ten hours each day I spent working at my job. Most of the struggles of my working day became a routine over time – one which I had little control over and did what I could, given the circumstances. There was a "go, go, go" attitude that didn't seem to stop. This works fine until life gives you a new challenge.

I learned when we had our first child that the life I knew had changed and would continue to change. After we raised three kids, life changed again and we could begin enjoying the empty nest with a carefree attitude. Now after so many years of post-child rearing, I actually think about grandchildren.

Many retirees spend a lot of time and energy with their grandchildren. They say it's fun to spend time with the kids and then give them back to their parents. As much as I looked forward to retirement I'm looking forward to grandkids in retirement. Right now, I'm feeling optimistic and happy-go-lucky.

Day 260 - Man's Best Friend or Dog's Best Friend

I've had a dog in my life for a long time. Her name is Scrappy. It's really my wife's dog and I act and behave with this in mind. Being retired has me interacting much more and I can't say who has benefited more. I'm not sure what percentage of retirees have dogs but I think more people have dogs today than years ago.

Not a day goes by where I live that I don't see a dog and its owner walking down the street. Some people have two dogs, and I also once had two dogs for a short time. Besides the companionship, I wonder how their personality is affected by their owners. Most people take very good care of their dog and they act reasonable around others. We take Scrappy sailing with us and she's been to the beach but I don't think she likes either one very much.

I think my wife enjoys the dog experience more than I do. She worked from home and has always spent a lot of time with Scrappy. I know why a dog is man's or woman's best friend. Since we retired Scrappy has never questioned our how, where and why of what we do. Everyone else seems to be more interested. Maybe retirement should be more of a dog's life.

Day 261 - Food for Thought

My grandmother lived to the age of 105. When she was 100, we had a big party at a restaurant. We rented a private room and everyone in the family was excited to celebrate such an unusual occasion. My grandmother was retired for forty years. Wow! That's a long time. I can't image.

As the evening wore on and family members began to leave the party, the wait staff, cooks and other restaurant workers came to the private area to meet my grandmother. They asked me if they could ask her some questions. By all means was my response and soon a waitress approached and asked her, "What was the most important thing in life?" My grandmother said, "You need to love yourself before you can love others."

Then after some startled looks a bus boy in line to speak with her asked, "What is the most important thing we should do in life?" Grandma answered without much thought, "Don't ask why, spend your time figuring out what you are going to do about it."

I never asked my grandmother such serious questions and was surprised with how quickly she answered. The last person in line, the head chef, was somewhat anxious. He introduced himself and asked if everything was satisfactory. We all agreed it was and my grandmother asked if he had a question for her. He said, "You have lived for one hundred years and have eaten many things so what did you eat that allowed you to live this long?" She replied, "My whole life I ate only one thing." We all looked puzzled and the chef asked, "What was that?" She looked at him and said, "Food."

Everyone laughed but the chef left the room and my grandmother said, "Enough questions. It's time to go home." Retirement can make you wiser if you ask the right questions. It can also help you maintain a sense of humor.

Day 262 - Are you Kidding?

I think retirees like jokes, fun times and kidding around. The last time I saw this much kidding around was in high school. Maybe in both cases some drinking was involved. The difference though is retirees don't need alcohol to start the process, they just need an audience. The laughter continues as more people join in and the material for the laughter is provided by the responses from the group.

My grandfather spent a lot of his time kidding with me and my friends. Practically every holiday or family occasion and get-together he made comments, asked silly questions and never responded to the looks of amazement and often disapproval.

He was from Poland but loved to ask you in Russian how you were. The greeting uses a word that sounds like "cock" which my grandfather didn't realize might offend someone. He also spoke some words in Italian and Arabic. I always laughed from the expressions on his victims. I wouldn't dare to follow my grandfather's example but I most certainly kid around more in retirement and anyone could be my target.

It's fun to see their responses, and I have nothing to lose. I begin with a greeting, maybe a joke, then I start the kidding around. The more people the better because others may join in. People remember a happy-go-lucky person. I think it's a good role for retirees.

Day 263 - Rise to the Occasion

It's not easy to rise to the occasion when you are retired. It could be you're not willing or able and you don't have the interest like you once did. Going out on the dance floor for some of us makes us uncomfortable. Any number of excuses work, and no one will force you to do anything.

This privilege comes with old age but acting like a bump on a log doesn't allow for much fun to take place. I also stress the importance of setting an example for those who are younger as they are the ones who will take your place. I once heard it explained this way, "You can't choose the music at a wedding you're at but you can decide on how you are going to dance." I may be assuming you will dance but think of it as participating and everyone will enjoy your efforts.

Many retirees dance every chance they get. When I watch these individuals, they are very competent and I wish I had what they had. Most of us will agree that the way to rise to any occasion is to be prepared. Getting your attitude or frame of mind set will get you past the first step. It's the hardest step to learn but the most important.

Once you tell yourself to have a good time you are ready for the next step. Do what others are doing and no one will notice. If you start break dancing, be prepared for competition. Participating and rising to the occasion is beneficial for all of us who witness the event. It becomes part of the memories you create and share. Your example is very important!

Day 264 - Direction

I went to a Feng Shui class today and didn't know anything about it except that practitioners put things in a specific direction or location to take advantage of energy forces and harmonize with their surroundings. As I approach the three quarters mark of retirement this first year in retirement, I'm also asking myself what direction am I going and why I have chosen it?

My grandmother told me not to ask why but concentrate on what you are going to do about anything and everything that's a concern, problem or option. I'm open to discovery, learning and expanding my knowledge in foreign practices.

Feng Shui is thousands of years old and practiced in many cultures. After the introduction to this topic I passed on more training. I'll follow some new directions and maybe rethink my surroundings first. I also went to a psychic fair not too long ago and realized this stuff exists for the curious to explore. I'm happy to report it all serves for the betterment of mankind.

A road map of life sounds like a good idea. Maybe our society now relies too much on GPS. I believe science can't explain everything. Do you put your trust in the unknown or the unfamiliar? My retirement journey is being shared for others to benefit and I can only hope we share in our destination. I'm enjoying the ride because I got new tires and a full tank of gas for the trip.

Day 265 - Effort

Can you go full bore in retirement? This is a race car term for as fast as possible. How about the expression half-assed, look this one up for fun? These are two expressions that my generation uses and they are opposites. I would describe my retirement as slow going, see what's out there, be open minded, try anything, show enthusiasm and make an honest effort to have a happy experience.

Before I go ahead with anything, I must get past the resistance all the efforts take. There is time and money involved but you don't have to commit too much of either one to make the effort worthwhile. I play pickleball and play a musical instrument often because I enjoy them and they are realistic, low investment options.

My effort was based on a need and reinforced with experience. You know you can't have a flame without a fire and you can't have a fire without a desire. I look forward to progress and the many encouragements I receive from friends and family. My motivation is simply to keep trying and believing that I may be able to offer others the same encouragement given to me. Making an effort and succeeding is a blessing.

Day 266 - Enter to Win

I like to think I may win a prize if I enter a contest. I've never asked other retirees if they feel the same way or if they enter contests only based on the prize. I have noticed though that at most gatherings of retirees in which there is an enter to win bowl, it's pretty full and there's a line of people waiting to enter. The contest sponsor probably feels the incentive of a prize will make giving over personal information easier. Of course, the sponsor is just trying to develop a contact list for later use.

In my many years of entering contests I have won a DVD player, $500 cash gift card and, most notably, a Grand Tour of Spain, all expenses paid plus cash spending money. People do win this stuff as I can attest. I rarely play the lottery but often see retirees buying tickets. I like the prize idea but not the odds.

I prefer enter to win contests and don't mind the exchange of information. How do I deal with the phone calls, emails and junk mail? I seem to get them whether or not I enter a contest. I'm fascinated with the idea of chance. I see the chance as an opportunity, it's there to take, it's my choice and you won't win unless you participate. I think of it as the opposite of fear of the unknown. The anticipation is more than worth the disappointment of not winning because someone did win. If you're smart, you'll also realize there will be another chance. Just wait and see.

Day 267 - A Piece of the Action

I've started selling stuff on eBay and at auction. I didn't have to sell anything but it was time to reduce my worldly possessions. I did most of the work myself including the listings, descriptions, packing and shipping and accounting.

My first discovery was how everyone involved was getting a piece of the action. Sometimes you have to pay fees or a percentage of the cost. Sometimes both. Some of these were fair but when I sold something for $300, after the expenses, I only received about $120.

It was time to reevaluate. This type of procedure took place when we bought and sold our home. When you think about it, every time you buy or sell something, there's some fees or taxes and other expenses that you may not have considered.

Commissions, administration costs, retainers and call it what you want, it's our way of doing business. Retirees need to be aware of this if they aren't already and should be prepared to receive less than they might have originally thought.

The other lesson I learned is if you raise your prices to cover all the expenses, you may not sell the item at all. The best advice I can give is to just be happy knowing that you have enjoyed your possession and now someone else will.

Day 268 - Watching the News

Many things happen to others whether we know it or not. During retirement I continue to watch the news, read newspapers, magazines and of course search the Internet. I think I spend more time doing this because I have the time and am truly interested in the ways of the world.

I wouldn't call myself a news junky but my moderate involvement is more than I expected in retirement. I find almost anything interesting and can discuss with others to come to a better understanding. I've learned some folks have an agenda, aren't very informed or just like to share views without substance. My mission in retirement is to continue looking at more than one side of the story and add my views when it's appropriate.

Some retirees are not interested in the news of the day unless it relates to their specific concerns, for example, social security and healthcare. When you consider retirees around the world, we don't all share the same benefits, treatment or respect that I think we deserve. I learned this by reading the news.

I would like to say that I'm not set in my ways, one sided or only concerned about myself. But through what I learn from the news and other sources, I have developed my own perspective. Being informed and sharing my perspective with whoever will listen, helps me understand how I fit in.

Retirees may not be the ones to change the world but they should stay informed about what's happening in the world.

Day 269 - Pastimes and Hobbies

I've never had many pastimes because I, like most people, was busy raising a family and working my business. As things progressed -- empty nest, sold my business and retired to Florida -- I began to rediscover all the pastimes available that I never pursued.

I've had hobbies, and pastimes aren't much different except for the time, money and effort you give them. Reading a magazine can be a pastime and reading in general can be a hobby. Pastimes are attractive to retirees because we don't have a set schedule, they often don't incur much expense and we can enjoy them with or without others. Sometimes I see it as playtime for adults.

I've seen a lot of retirees playing games inside and out. Our neighborhood newsletter lists over thirty activities. Each one is made up of enthusiastic individuals who want to share the time and activity with others. Even after all these months, I am still discovering and considering my own participation and may add something to the list. What do you like to do to pass the time?

Day 270 - Shallow Outcomes with Deep Thoughts

I have been known to ponder a lot and think about each and every day with gratitude, puzzlement and awe. These sentiments have increased because many people I knew are gone.

Retirees face daily questions such as, "Should I get a new something" or "Will the old one last," "Whom have I forgotten about," "What are my extended family members up to," "What can I do to help others or even myself?" I don't mean to dwell on death or even appear morbid but I'm honest about my time left on earth.

My wife says you don't know so don't worry so much. I agree but these thoughts are part of my decision-making. I often try to get more for less and forget that with the effort it takes I may be cheating myself out of time and energy. You may think something is a good idea but the justification may only make sense to you. In other words, doing what you want to do, may take you away from doing something that could have had a more positive effect on others.

Money is not the root of evil for retirees; instead it's the lack of money. In fact, lack of money and how to spend what you have becomes part of almost any discussion as it is foremost in most retirees' minds.

I learned long ago there are only three reasons for money -- to spend, save and share with others. Do you think you would be more generous if you had more money? I do. In fact, I think I would do more of everything if I had more money. But I have to admit that on occasion, I've pretended to not have money when I did. It's a character defect that needs attention.

Some of these deep thoughts result in shallow outcomes. What you think and what you do will change with experience. Many so-called good ideas or intentions are based on what you think you know. You may not be the one to answer your own questions. Seeking advice in retirement isn't second guessing, rather it allows you to find the motivation to be successful and share the time and money you have.

Day 271 - When is the Right Time?

I continue to read about retirement from articles in the newspaper, mail I receive and from the Internet. I started my retirement at age 63 and, for whatever reason, the media has made me feel a little guilty about not waiting until full retirement age of 66.

According to one article, only 37% of US workers retire from full-time jobs and stay retired. Some 14% retire to part-time jobs and 25% continue to work full or part-time past age 70. All I'm going to say is good for them, because I believe if you can afford not to have a job, being retired is the best choice after working a lifetime.

You should concentrate on health not wealth and retire with purpose. A lot of what I've read and heard I consider to be complete nonsense, unusual points of view and opinions that I wish I could argue in great detail.

For those of you who have to work, can't imagine not working and need a reason to get up in the morning please give yourself a chance to continue reading this journal. All too many opinions, different situations and needs dictate your choices.

Why not believe me when I say the sooner you retire the better. I love retirement and am a believer in doing what's best for you, first. I won't advise anyone to retire at any stage of life but I will assure you there is life after leaving your job. Choose wisely!

Day 272 - Make it Count

There are challenges in retirement I have experienced which are more difficult for me to overcome, and making progress on changing my personality defects is slow. People, I believe do change, but it may be harder to teach an old dog new tricks. I want all my efforts to count towards benefiting myself or others. Going through the motions is not something I like to do and it's easy to recognize when my heart is not into what I am doing.

I've seen retirees doing things just to keep busy without any care or real interest in their actions. If my goal is to be a competent musician, I think I should learn about music, practice and be honest about the results I am achieving. If paying for lessons is possible it may expedite the experience. It's always reasonable to pay for advice or lessons but retirees budget restraints or a lack of commitment may find it a convenient excuse not to.

For example, why should I take dance lessons or golf lessons? I'll never attain a great level. That's a bad attitude and you are denying yourself the experience. If you do want to make it count, follow the advice of the instructors or experts.

My wife had a personal trainer to help her get started on the road to exercise and now takes other classes as well. I think it has benefited her tremendously. We are all going to be reluctant in the beginning and face some disappointment. "You won't know until you try," was something I heard when I started my business that I ran for thirty years.

The ups and downs in any activity will strengthen your character and this is something no one can ever take away from you. I never saw failure as an option and I survived many obstacles. Retirement has none of these serious concerns but it's still up to you to make it worthwhile and count.

Day 273 - Caution to the Wind

I like sharing all the different expressions I've heard throughout my life. I moved to Iowa in my thirties and brought some Chicago expressions with me. Living in Florida now, I refer to any and all the expressions I've learned from both places. I also look forward to new ones whenever others speak.

Today I heard an old one – "Be careful or you'll be sorry." I thought I was cautious but as you age and find yourself retired; it may be wise to accept your new status. I always wear a life jacket when doing water sports, but maybe I should wear a bike helmet on my bike rides. I always use a seat belt in the car but sometimes drive too fast?

Sounds like common knowledge and why risk anything? I'm slow to accept my aging and abilities. I answered the question of what's the purpose of retirement -- a retirement of purpose. In the past I may have thrown caution to the wind. In retirement, it's time to get honest with yourself. I'm still hesitant to admit that I may need to be more cautious than I have been in the past. Changing my attitude is slow going for me, but I'm working on it.

Day 274 - It Can Be Unique

I'm off to another greatly anticipated trip to visit family. We are going on more trips than I thought possible considering we've had plenty of visitors and my wife only recently retired.

This trip is particularly important because today, we are going to meet our future son-in-law's parents who live in England. We have each day planned with some unique experiences in San Francisco. My wife warned me about having to go along with the crowd and making it as comfortable as possible for all involved.

The group dynamics will have to be experienced day-by-day. Day and night time activities may slow us old timers down, but I'm looking so forward to it. Nothing will stop me from enjoying each moment. One of the first things I learned about my son-in-law's dad was he retired at age 50 and has been retired for 20 years. I can't wait to ask him some retirement questions.

After meeting my son-in-law's dad, he proved to be living a full life, enjoying each day as if he only recently retired. He stressed that each retirement is unique and to make the most of it and keep it that way, do what you find worthwhile.

He loves scuba diving and each year goes on a three-week trip to explore the underwater world. He and his spouse have an arrangement or agreement as he put it to each pursue their own passions. I can't imagine not seeing my wife for three weeks and being able to afford such a trip every year.

He spoke with joy and was so enthusiastic about life, I want what he has. His one piece of advice made the trip memorable. We, upon parting, mentioned each of our spouses had recently retired and each of us was curious as to what each of them would choose to do. Time will tell.

Day 275 - Make It A Big Deal If You Want

We are having a big dinner tonight with a birthday celebration and meeting some new folks. I've been accused of making a big deal about everything and parties are perfect for a splurge. I've even acted like retirement is a big deal and it helps me to justify my actions or lack of actions.

I've tried to downplay my retirement and go unnoticed but I get enjoyment from choosing to make it a big deal. Each activity gets my full attention but with not much retirement experience, I'm learning to show just enough enthusiasm to let others know I really enjoy my retirement and all it has to offer.

To contrast with this thought, sometimes I think what if is my last chance or opportunity to enjoy the experience. I remind myself none of us knows the future so don't think that way. I try to appear level-headed and calm but I'm just so excited about everything. What can I do to make this dinner party memorable and why stop there? Let's make all of retirement enjoyable. It is a big deal!

Day 276 - Go Along for The Ride

I have seen many retirees not take retirement too seriously and I categorize it as going along for the ride. It's not totally aimless, it's just that these retirees may not be following their true purpose for what they have chosen to do.

I've asked many retirees how retirement is going and many times I get the same response, "It's great." When I add, "What have you been doing lately?" The answers don't come easy. If you're just going along for the ride, I have to ask, "Who's doing the driving?"

Today I took a car full of family members for a long ride to do some sightseeing. I was excited and content to go on this ride because we were sharing an experience. Our journey involved some wine tasting so I was the designated driver. There were two back seat drivers and three navigators to make for an interesting ride. I'm not sure if it was my age, status as a retiree or past experience, but no one was interested in what I had to say and they preferred perhaps that I just did the driving.

Maybe if I had only one passenger, I could have had a better conversation. I think it was funny that I was given the task of driving both ways to the wine tasting and no one volunteered to drive to the venue. They gave me the task but didn't trust me to fulfill my responsibility.

I came to the conclusion that if I did a good job, I would gain some trust. If I was better prepared, we would all enjoy the journey. It sounds like it's the same for retirement. If you choose to go along for the ride, be prepared to answer some questions.

Day 277 - Bring Some Culture into Your Life

We spent most of today visiting cultural places like museums. There were a variety of people at each place we visited and I noticed an older crowd. They seemed to be willing to spend the time to read any labels and were observing at a slow and deliberate pace. I love going to museums and could spend all day wandering the halls and discovering the permanent and traveling exhibits.

In each entrance to the museums I noticed a display of important donors who helped make the place possible. Many museums offer discounts to seniors and many seniors like to become members. It offers you a discount and you're donating to a good cause. The knowledge and cultural understanding as well as the entertainment value are well worth the time and money.

I would suggest taking a tour whenever possible. It provides an introduction and allows you to become familiar with the exhibits. Many retirees volunteer at these places and can meet other retirees who share a common interest.

Each place we visited had a gift shop and a place to eat. After today's experience I decided I enjoyed the place as well as seeing all the people who were also there. Retirees like to go out and about. I'd put museums on the top of my list.

Day 278 - New Sights

I've never traveled somewhere and then gone somewhere else afterward. Usually you go on vacation and then return home. Extending our travels like we are, going first to San Francisco and then onto Portland has made me even more energized. Two very different places and different people will make for interesting conversations when we get home.

Retirement has offered us an extended holiday visiting with friends and family. We don't have any worries other than what's convenient for those we are visiting. We can add a day or two to any journey. Careful planning is still helpful but why pass up an opportunity if you make a discovery of interest. I even thought, what if we continue on to a third or fourth destination?

Giving yourself the chance to experience some new sights sometimes happens just because you're there to make those discoveries. I'd suggest trying it sooner rather than later. I think I waited too long to not see how great it was to be heading out for a second adventure without going home first.

Day 279 - Catching Up

Retirement has been the best time to catch up with family and friends. As long as the time you have is mutual then you will be able to fulfill each other's needs. You'll catch up and soon be able to plan ahead. Wouldn't it be nice to have something to look forward to? You can exchange suggestions and offer ideas with a time and place and remind everyone how flexible you are in retirement.

If I know I'll see someone again based on our conversation, it's a happy feeling. The times I say good-bye and don't know when I'll see someone again are sometimes sad for me. Retirement shouldn't be a sad time so I suggest we make more things happen.

A casual phone call or e-mail can begin the process. If they are too busy or not interested, don't feel put off. When things do work out and you are away from home together, it's usually a good time to share what's going on in your lives and plan where and when to meet up again. Some kind words and a lot of encouragement will fulfill your wishes.

Day 280 - A Long Hike Won't Let You Down

We went on a three-hour hike today that was tough and more than I can usually handle without some preparation. I like to challenge myself in retirement and this was just the kind of thing I recommend for everyone. The walk was up hill to see some waterfalls. I soon learned that if you ever start feeling down just climb a hill or go to someplace with a view. You'll feel a sense of accomplishment and you may start to see things differently.

Making that effort isn't easy but it starts with the first step. You may even meet others who are doing the same thing. It's interesting to learn what has motivated others to do the hike at the same time you are. Oftentimes you find out that, although you have a common goal, we have different reasons for completing the challenge.

In this particular case the journey and destination were equally important. My brother told me that if you want to see the waterfall you must climb the hill. It sounded profound for a second and then I questioned whether or not I was prepared?

Proper shoes and water were my main concerns. On the way down from the hilltop I felt some relief and accomplishment. To my surprise I was passed up by a young man without a water bottle who was not wearing shoes on the rocky trail. Wow! I wasn't just surprised, I was shocked!

I know I won't forget seeing the waterfalls after the tough climb and that young man without shoes made me realize how old I really am. Tomorrow we go home and I'm already thinking about coming back and doing the same hike. I bet that next time I'll think about it a lot differently.

Day 281 - Forward and Back

We spent all day traveling back home. I spent a lot of time going over the details of each part of each day. As I did the recall over and over, more details became important. It was like I was telling my brain to try to remember as much as possible. Even as many times and as long as I took to go over and over these details, the time still went by fast.

I've been having the same back and forth thoughts about retirement too! I don't consider retirement new. When I compare my working life to my retired life, I realize there is a lot more variety in what I do today. I know it's up to me to continue trying more activities but I'm also conscious of not doing too many.

Today, I'm not as content with each day being the same. There's a routine, but I can change anything I want. I remind myself that retirement is time for enjoyment, relaxation and fun-loving action. If that's not happening then I'm doing something wrong.

There's a serious side as well and I'm aware that retirees deal with illness, loneliness and death. It's all about life on life's terms. I know we can't foresee much and each of us can only control how we respond to adversity.

I certainly dwell on details and go back and forth in my thoughts. I have learned in retirement to listen more to others and then attempt to understand the different options. I always learn more when I listen than when I speak.

Day 282 - Take a Break

I usually feel motivated each day to do something necessary and useful. Our seven days away made me aware that my "catching up on home chores sooner than later attitude" is waning. I find myself taking more breaks and not fussing about getting everything done. I think my wife sees it as second guessing what I set out to do. It's laundry, grocery shopping and yard work for me today.

I usually feel rejuvenated after a vacation and want that feeling to last as long as possible. Many times, I've gotten back into the routine and wondered if I even went on a vacation? The idea of retirement being a permanent vacation may sound good; but it's not true. Maybe with more practice I'll get the hang of it.

Money and budgeting have been the mainstay of most of my actions. I continue to remind myself that it is okay to take a break. I am constantly evaluating what I need, what I want and what I am thinking. What better time to reflect on these things than during a break?

Day 283 - Why Bother?

I once read that each experience makes us who we are today. The older we get and the more experiences we have, the more unique we become. My recent vacation got me wondering what difference it makes if I review and question the how, what, where and why. My wife seems to move ahead easily and is on to the next task. What you did is over, so just move on.

Retirement is like a book because there's a story to tell and you're the writer. I know some folks write memoirs about their past before they even reach retirement. But I am seeing my retirement as another chapter that needs to be experienced before I would consider writing my memoir.

I guess what I find worthwhile are the simple things that are ahead of me like the salad I'm making for dinner tonight. With more choices I think I'll have better results. My actions aren't to impress anyone including myself but rather to take the time to make them count.

I've had many rushed conversations and they held little importance. Now in retirement I continue to enjoy the time to engage even in simple tasks like making a salad. Many retirees like to stay in a comfortable state and no longer want to engage in tedious tasks, arduous conversations, but prefer to relax with the satisfaction of a job well done. I'm becoming more and more that way with everything I do. Sometimes I think, "Why bother."

Day 284 - First Impressions

I heard a sermon about first impressions today. Sure, we've all heard the expression, "You don't get a second chance to make a first impression." This sermon centered on the order of the things people notice during the first impression.

One reason for our recent trip was to meet our daughter's future in-laws. I really didn't think about what impression I made until hearing this sermon. I need several encounters and discussions with others before I can articulate my impression of them. I know my daughter was more concerned at the time than I and maybe it was her age that made her anxious for the best outcome.

Retirement doesn't give you any excuses for making a poor first impression. Do you present your gender, age and status first? What is the first thing others see in you? Can you make an effort that is honest without too much precaution?

The preacher asked many more questions which gave me many more things to think about. Most retirees represent themselves as reasonable, polite and kind individuals. We are an older group with many different life experiences and tend to mingle with those most familiar to us. The preacher said our views happen simultaneously. You can alter this going forward.

While you are thinking all of these things about those you meet, they are also thinking many things about you. He suggested we surprise each other with the best impression and I couldn't agree more. Amen!

Day 285 - Where Have You Been? Where Are You Going?

I got back to meeting up with my pickleball buddies and was asked where I had been? All of them are retired and they notice if you're not around. After a brief rundown of where I'd been, what I saw and what I did, the conversation switched to where we'd be going in the near future.

All of us had plans on going somewhere for some reason. We shared similar life experiences and had educational, economic and practical similarities. Yet each of us chose different places based on our time and budgets.

I'm not surprised at the varying directions and find it common in retirement to travel and enjoy the world we haven't seen and do the things we'd like to do. None of us has a defined retirement, rather an accepted expectation to enjoy our retirements any way we choose.

Retirees like to do many different things and share many of them with others. I don't really have a bucket list, but rather a "do the most you can with what you have" attitude It's our deserved retirement, we earned it. I'm going to Chicago next, how about you?

Day 286 - Confidence

Do you know how well you are doing at any particular activity? I'm a really enthusiastic dulcimer player, learning all I can to improve. I had a gig that was fun and it gave me a confidence boost. Whenever I turn my attention to retirement, I try to look for the same thing. I've covered what's important, starting out with trying new things, evaluating the results and deciding if I want to continue to learn more.

Confidence is by far the one element I need to constantly address because it doesn't last long. Sometimes days and even sometimes hours go by and I second-guess myself. I'm still reflecting on my Oregon five-mile hike last week. I was happy to complete it, but can't get the young man I saw doing the hike without shoes out of my mind.

It is totally impossible for me to comprehend. What does he have, where did he get it and will I ever find it? I once watched the great guitarist Carlos Santana explain what you need to channel to be a great musician. It's about having the confidence and conviction of the body, mind and spirit. You need all three!

Prayer and meditation bring together these three elements and I'm trying to practice this more often. If you're wondering why you need confidence, it's simply the way to bring enthusiasm into your life. I certainly will never amount to a musician like Santana and I'll never hike five miles without shoes, but never underestimate an old man with a dulcimer.

Day 287 - Illness

My first encounter with illness in five years and also the first in retirement has knocked me out. It must be food poisoning because after a few hours of not feeling well, I've recovered and appear fine. It immediately reminded me of how easy it is to forget about your wellbeing.

How healthy am I and what will it take to get me to see a doctor? Once a year should do it, right? Many folks are surprised I don't take any medications. Seldom do I have any headaches. My knee is about my biggest concern. I certainly believe there is more to come. During many pickleball games I play, I'll size up my opponent or partner and assess their age and general condition.

I'm first and foremost grateful for being able to play. It's a healthy, not too strenuous or damaging sports activity for older folks like me. I have convinced myself that staying active reduces my chances of getting some illness. I see the importance of water intake and rest, but I've overdone it many times. I just love the game!

Illness can be a serious situation at any age but recovery time is greatly increased as you get older. I'm practicing the three "R's" each day -- retirement, rest and relaxation.

Day 288 - Speak Up!

I received a notice that our neighborhood was facing some new development and we needed to attend a community meeting and speak up about our concerns. I will be happy to attend and giving my opinion on any familiar topic is what I do best. My shyness went away before retirement but now this gives all of us who attend a chance to make a difference.

I've been to general meetings before for a variety of reasons and have observed that many of those who are outspoken don't actually address the concerns of the group, but rather their own needs. As a group of homeowners, our purpose as I see it is to retain a safe, quiet environment with less traffic.

As a group of retired homeowners, we want what we have to remain the same and feel we are entitled to be protected from commercialism. I've held the belief that if you don't like something be verbal and express your concerns with some concrete solutions. Delivering a message or expressing your opinion is easy. Helping others see and value of what we need, want or expect is not.

Day 289 - Words and Actions

I did a lot of talking yesterday and hope my words can turn into some action. Today I'm more interested in catching up on some newspaper reading. I read the newspaper four days a week and have for many years. If I don't get to a newspaper on the day of delivery, I'll still keep the paper and read it a day or two later.

I get to examine many local and worldly occurrences from the comfort of my home. I especially look for anything related to retirement, aging, health and contemporary issues, which have held my interest since my college days.

I will admit, I also very often read the obituaries and am fascinated with other people's lives. Many times, I reflect on what my own obituary would say if I wrote it myself vs. someone in my family. Many of the stories of these folks include what the individual did after retiring. If someone had a long obituary, I would give it more attention because I liked to compare what they did before retirement to their after-retirement activities.

I also like to read the phrases that an individual says often enough that family members remember them for it. Two I recall are, "That will be the day" and "Are you kidding me?"

Today I read about an engineer who used to say, "How's that working out for you?" I find that at times that my words are not always reflected in my actions. My retirement slogan has been, "Hey! What do you expect? I'm retired." After all this newspaper reading, I'm ready to get off my duff and turn my words into action.

Day 290 - Put That in Your Pipe and Smoke It

It seems like alcohol and marijuana use are more common in retirement than I thought. It's not an issue with me because I don't do either one. I've had my share of these and other vices in the past and can only say it probably did more harm than good. Both illness and idle time which older folks experience, can lead to self-medicating.

Retirees should be sure they are making an informed decision before partaking in either recreational or medical use of marijuana. Do those near and dear to you understand your actions and where they might lead. Many retirees laugh it off and say, "I've been there and done that." "It's ok, it's no big deal!"

I caution anyone with or without experience, drugs and alcohol are more potent at an older age. I'm less nonchalant and will give out warnings to anyone I care about. My advice, if you can handle it, is to do it in moderation. In retirement that means everything. Drugs, sex and rock-n-roll will always be available. We're now old enough to know better and still young enough to care.

Day 291 - Making Predictions

For some reason I've started to like making predictions. It's a challenge to my intellect and I have no particular skill in this regard but retirement has me thinking about what I know and don't know.

It's an amusement to make bold statements without much information. When I watch TV shows or sporting events, I'll make a prediction about the outcome. When it comes to family members and their lives unfolding, I'll state the good and bad possible outcomes. I'm not intuitive, psychic or mean-spirited but rather I like testing some unknown and wishful ability to see things others don't.

Retirement has a similar cause and effect on me and my day-to-day decisions. I think I know a lot more than I did before, but there is a need to make sense of it all. No one cares about my predictions and I don't get challenged. About the best record I have is with predicting weather. I have studied weather with interest and have achieved some appreciated skills. I see the ebb and flow of weather and apply it to retirement.

Retirement isn't about not working or just fun and games. Each day brings new surprises, delights, challenges, opportunities and predictable outcomes. If I forget to set the alarm and I play it by ear it may not be as good of a day and I may not like the outcome. I am not one to play craps or throw dice, but I have been known to play roulette and win often.

Day 292 - Get What You Want

Do you get what you want? In restaurants I see what looks good and doesn't cost too much. I may on my birthday or anniversary say to myself and guests, "Get what you want, it's a celebration." I am also of the mindset that if I think something costs too much, I won't get it no matter what the situation or desire.

Being retired has me trying to break this old habit and not be so tight with money. I should accept and understand there is a cost of providing a good or service.

I wanted to win today at pickleball. I was determined to get what I wanted. But it didn't happen. Now I see it's more important to understand how you act or feel when you don't get what you want.

Do adults act like children? All the time. If retirement ends up less than you expected you may have to ask others what they think happened. Sometimes you get lost in your desires and need to focus on life on life's terms.

Do you know what you will do if things don't work out? I've often said that lowering your expectations is part of life when you're a mature human being. Getting what you need can make you grateful. Many times, I've decided in many situations people don't really know what they want.

Day 293 - Too Much is Too Much!

There is more to retirement than I expected. Each and every week I hear, read and experience the many options, activities and attitudes of retirees. They continue to see what else is out there and what else they can do.

Maybe I'm around some overachievers who were this way before retirement but maybe retirement has brought this out in them. I often can't keep up. I'm not complaining but rather asking when is too much too much? I know it's different for each of us but I choose to have fewer quality experiences rather than several hurried experiences.

I'd like to achieve a level of proficiency and then move on to other things. I'm concentrating on doing four or five things well and see quality over quantity as my goal. If I ask myself would I like to spend a month traveling in Spain or go to several national parks in the US, I'd say I want to do both. But, can I do both?

The way to answer this for me is to say this year I'll do this, and next year I'll try that. I'm not going to sit on my front porch and watch the world go by either. Right now, I'm thinking I should water the lawn or wash my car. I know now I can do both.

Day 294 - Agenda

It's Wednesday and my routine has my wife asking, what's on your agenda today? She's only been retired for about three months and already has an agenda six days a week. I bet women are more organized than men.

For me it's mid-week so I'm open without one single thing in mind. I don't often find myself in this situation and I'd rather have more structure for each day of the week. Even just one option that doesn't take much time or planning would help.

I think having something to look forward to is very important in retirement. When I was working, I had a boy's night out on Thursdays that I looked forward to and was content to just have, with or without plans. Each weekend was a balance of chores and fun family time.

Everyone tells you it's good to keep busy when you retire but they don't go as far as telling you what to do. Retirement doesn't have or need a specific agenda but I think you'll do more and enjoy the outcome if you consider one.

Day 295 - Use It or Lose It

Today I didn't wake up thinking about the day ahead of me but rather I questioned why I didn't do much yesterday. It didn't bother me too long as I realized I can't go back in time. I recalled the saying, "Yesterday is history, tomorrow a mystery, but today is a gift, that is why we call it the present."

To that, I've added, use it or lose it. I may feel as if I should make up for yesterday by doing more today. I should be able to even things out if I choose to. I think I've developed a retirement consciousness. I felt this way about spending each day productively before I retired. I've also made myself act like a role model for other retirees.

If I assume a nonchalant approach, I may lose the time and never be able to make it up. What's more important? I never thought retirement would have such an affect on me.

Some retirees just fill up time, even with activities that they have said they don't like. If you are going to spend the day not doing much, you might want to question your motives, honestly.

Day 296 - Isolation

I do consider some of the serious sides of retirement when I encounter them. I try to remain aware and don't want life just passing me by. There are retirees who find themselves in isolation as situations change in their lives. Old age, death of a spouse and social insecurities are some of the causes. I think men may become more isolated than women but there are also fewer of us as we age.

The social group I'm in hasn't suffered from isolation, but they do mention their other family members and even their moms and dads being isolated and lonely. If you find yourself in a similar state, be aware of the risks. These include depression, illness, diminished comprehension, drug and alcohol abuse, high blood pressure and perhaps even early death.

In one of my meetings, news about missing members travels fast and we try to reach out and offer help. It's all about learning to cope and adjusting to new circumstances. We often lose ambition and passion and become forlorn.

We should consider sharing the time we have together and recognizing many of us are out there that could use some encouragement. Reaching out and feeling reluctant is to be expected. I ask, "What if it were me," and recognize that I can make a difference.

Day 297 - Museum Day

My wife and I decided to go to another museum today. We spent the whole day on this trip because it was out of town and the special exhibit was as interesting as the museum itself. The experience was a look back in history and the exhibits gave us an insight as to how we got to where we are today.

Retirement has given us a better opportunity to explore interesting and new sights. We never hurry anymore because of some expectation. The leisurely museum trip gave us a newfound way of spending the day. It offers an easy come, easy go way of living. This was the fourth museum we visited during retirement, but it was our first all-day activity. We had an in-depth need to learn about what we saw and were devoted to staying as long as it took.

Savoring the moment and place in time has shown me how details can help explain life and its changes. This venue is both entertaining and informative if you're willing to slow the process.

I think books and movies can help introduce a topic but exhibits bring to life the subject matter. The real objects in front of you help you to focus on what they're about. I don't think I've ever thought about washing my car or mowing the lawn when I was at a museum.

Retirees can enjoy the experience, expand a horizon and even offer some insight. If you want it to be more worthwhile give it more time. Explore more, work less!

Day 298 - Sentimental Seniors

I spent the morning playing music, my second gig, for a group of senior citizens all retired and many years older than me. Each of them had years of experience with retirement and I wish I could have interviewed them all.

The kindness and gratitude our music group received was outstanding. The conversations before and after our show definitely showed me how the sentiments of the elderly change during the advancement of each decade.

Starting in the fifties and continuing with the sixties, seventies and eighties, each group has a new perspective, more experience and offers more gratitude. The cycle of life becomes more of a reality. When I see young children I often wonder if and when I will be a grandfather? My skepticism of the youth and compassion for others has already changed. Perhaps seeing this in older adults has made me aware of my own future and destiny.

Being aware of the changes and what they bring or take away may help me adapt or adjust better. I don't think anyone would say I'm kind, compassionate and caring. I do however feel the need to become these things. A nice life in retirement comes with knowing this and keeping tabs on your emotions and sentiments.

Day 299 - Learn Your Lesson

I spend most of my time playing sports, practicing and learning my music and pursuing interests like gardening. I watch videos, read books, talk about them with others and go to class or other formal instructional activities. My goal is to improve and without this goal I lose interest very quickly. Soon this may change but until then I'm all about progress not perfection!

No one is teaching me retirement and I continue to learn on my own. I have read about it, observed it in others, talked about it with those willing to listen and now I am writing about it.

The one thing I haven't done is give myself or received a grade on how well I'm doing. Have I learned my lesson or is it time to move onto other lessons from qualified individuals with more experience?

I think during this first year of retirement you should branch out and try new things. It's easier to look at each activity as a new experience which may or may not suit you. You won't know until you try it and whether or not you like it, be honest with yourself.

I'm doing a few things to gain some confidence and ability before I'm claiming to be a jack of all trades and master of none. I have thought about becoming a master gardener and can't tell you why. I guess I need to learn my other lessons before I take on any more classroom work.

Day 300 - Contradictions

When you retire, how you retire, where you retire, and with whom you retire makes all the difference in the world. Sometimes I feel like I'm on the retirement train, people are going places, some get off and others get on. We share our experiences, give warnings about our discoveries and look forward to our different destinations.

When we buy our first ticket, it's a one-way fare and only after we reach our first destination and get off the train can we buy another ticket to somewhere else. The only other option is to return home. Eventually we run out of money, time, or our health gives out and our train ride comes to an end.

I didn't dream this but feel this way about retirement. There are two other main concerns on this train ride. We can look out the window and visit with our fellow travelers or we can cover the window and not engage with anyone.

This contradiction of being on the same train yet not seeing or doing what others have in mind makes me think, "Maybe you should have stayed home." You can however, also invite others along on your trip. I think most individuals will appreciate you thinking about them and including others makes for a shared experience. I don't see any contradictions, do you?

Day 301 - Constant Communications

We all have many electronic gadgets to stay in constant communication. Each and every activity or group I'm involved with has email, Facebook and general phone outreach almost on a daily basis. If you want to know anything or want to provide information you just press some buttons. You still can't make anyone open their computer or answer their phone, but it's the main way we communicate.

I did once recently have someone come to my house and talk to me uninvited. I had forgotten what that was like. Are we all so busy in retirement that we need to have this constant communication? Being informed, staying active and sharing our experiences is what I like, but how about trying to say what needs to be said in public.

Do our physical encounters appear friendlier than electronic communications? Do we communicate in detail in person or relegate that to electronic devices? I like the ease of communication but think too much is not being said in person.

Articles I read say kids are buried in their communication devices but I think it's affected everyone including retirees. I'm unplugged today and will test if I can last more than one day.

Day 302 - Legalize It

Those who are able to retire do so because they can afford it. All the financial planning has taken place, we've estimated, budgeted and adjusted and our spending. How long it lasts and if it will last long enough is anyone's guess.

The next step should be to legalize it with some estate planning. Because of yesterday's seminar on retirement that I attended it's time to look at these assets and make sure they're protected. I probably should have known this and done it sooner. The stock market goes up and down, taxes don't go away, retirement may mean assisted living or nursing home care and you can never assume anything.

A revocable trust plan and a will is my next goal and should be part of everyone's retirement duties. I've enjoyed my ten-months of retirement, but realize that some things need to get done and there are consequences if you don't do them. Substantial money management has never been my forte but there are many individuals and businesses set up to help.

It's my money. Now I need to decide what I am going to do with it to provide for myself and my family? Estate Planning advice may cost some money but consider it an insurance policy that is well worth it. After a few hours of meeting with some advisors you'll still have time for a round of golf.

Day 303 - Ahh!

I can say I'm confident in my retirement and explain why it's important. Other times I want to just not worry about anything and say, "Ahh! Just enjoy each moment and be of service." That's the most important thing I've learned. Feeling well and free to participate in life comes with knowing anything can happen to change this.

I want to be part of something that has meaning, at least to me. Most of my early ideas I had when I retired are still true. I have begun to recognize and find new meaning in the things I choose to do. I told my son recently that I'm close to finalizing my latest gardening design and his response was, "Yah! Right Dad, I don't believe that for a minute."

I walk around my home and make observations and want it to be completed. I do the work myself and like it. I think I need more Ahh! moments and if it gets done it may be revised as I learn and see more. Sounds like my retirement may get even better, who knows?

Day 304 - Big Weekend

Three days until the end of summer has me reflecting on what I did this year. I know it's Florida and summer is almost year-round but even after five years here I think of Labor Day weekend as the end of summer. I don't put the grill away but I try to make sure it's super clean for the fall season. I do the same with my car when it comes to waxing it. I also think the cooler weather is the time to finish painting the front of the house.

Every one of these things in retirement is much easier to approach and complete because I see the value, have the time and experience to know the results. I have a "been there and done that," attitude.

This three-day weekend will allow for some chores and also some fun. I don't even worry about the order of things as long as it gets done. I only insist on variety in each week, weekend or holiday activity. I'm the opposite of laissez faire when it comes to expectations. The weather however is still a deciding factor in what I do.

Day 305 - Common Ground

All things are not equal in retirement. There are the haves and have nots. I knew this all along but retirement doesn't give you much chance to change this. Now, how and where you live provides insight into your state of mind, resources, interests, purpose and expectations. I like to think that all retirees are on common ground and share a common purpose. I'm not interested in worldly possessions or status in society. If you are happy doing what you like and sharing these experiences, then I respect and admire you. Unfortunately, I have run across some very judgmental retirees.

I approach everyone with a friendly handshake, fist bumps if you insist, hello followed by a comment or question to engage them. I've seen other sides and different approaches and am guilty of being insecure.

I don't know any super rich people. I stay grounded in my middle-class group. I wouldn't mind knowing some rich folks because they'd probably share some experiences I can't afford. We may not have much common ground but we can still learn from each other. I like most retirees and as a group, they are very nice to be with regardless of their economic background.

Day 306 - Caring for Others

You may choose to or be given the task of caring for others. Family comes first but it may be a friend or neighbor who needs your help. If you're retired, assistance is always welcome. Putting yourself out in the beginning is difficult. You may not know if you're willing and able and to what extent you'll be called upon. People may take advantage of your offer. It's up to you to decide what you can, will or won't do.

You may find it easier to help those who, through no fault of their own, need a helping hand. But, don't be too quick to judge. Once you decide to help one individual, family, friend or neighbor you may realize you become unavailable to help others. While those around you may admire your good deeds, they may also feel your absence.

Retirement and free time are not the same thing. Those not retired may think you don't work so you have the time to provide them what they think they need. The more elderly can ask, "What if it were you, what would you do?"

In some cases, someone else's problem now becomes your problem. Are you going to be part of the solution? I like to frame my involvement with, "Let's see how it works out." I have cared for others and lost my temper, got angry and was disappointed. I also had some of the greatest sharing experiences of my life.

Day 307 - Each Game is an Experience and Each Experience is a Game

I use the word "experience" to mean many different things. When I was working, my clients often used the word "project". They'd say, "I have a project for you." Retirement has brought me both. I think projects can be an experience and an experience can be a project. Why they end up being a game of sorts is anyone's guess.

I've met some smart folks in retirement who exhibit many skills, have leadership qualities and enjoy the retirement way of living. Some of them seem to turn it into a game in which there are winners and losers. If you are on their team, then you are considered a winner. The rules of these games aren't stated but once you encounter the experience, you'll have to decide for yourself if it's fair or not.

There aren't any rewards or prizes and you shouldn't need to brag about the results because it's not considered good sportsmanship. If your feelings get hurt you don't belong in the game. Those who choose to not participate usually say they don't find it amusing. Can you tell I just got back from three hours of playing pickleball?

Day 308 - Miracles and Magic

Just because you believe in something doesn't make it true, and not believing in something doesn't make it untrue. I like magic but I don't consider it a miracle. There are also some things in life that I would consider miracles. There could be some sort of divine intervention we just don't understand. It's not necessarily fate for each of us, but rather a destiny to be discovered or revealed.

Retirement could be a good time to examine all the strange and unfamiliar beliefs that are out there. I'd say reexamine a standard religious belief that you are familiar with first, and then go on to a relatively new spiritual idea. Your understanding or awareness of either one will expand your horizons.

We often wonder about how magic is created or possible. You can put some magic into your retirement, but don't expect any miracles. Magic is a just a trick. Miracles require divine intervention. It's easy to understand why non-believers would ask, with billions of people on earth, what makes someone so special that they would be singled out to receive a miracle.

My retirement isn't about miracles and the magic is really me doing things I enjoy. I'm basically a skeptic but I'm also childlike regarding the mysteries of this world. I often wish I could figure out the tricks of magic but soon realize I may not want to watch it if I knew how it was done.

I've never witnessed a miracle but I think the idea is a possibility. I encourage everyone to explore the spiritual ideas we seem to run into and go out and find some you never heard of. Keep an open mind. The fact that I've learned a thing or two in retirement isn't a miracle and I don't know how to do magic but I still get to wonder about each one and still appreciate the possibilities of both.

Day 309 - Security

The one thing in retirement which we all would like is security. Hopefully you are receiving social security. There are also other types of security that aren't financial, like when you're at home with your spouse in domestic bliss. We value security and self-preservation.

When I retired in Florida and was seeking a new home, I asked the realtor, "How far is the nearest hospital?" He asked if I had a condition or concern and my wife told him it's just my insecurities. I still lock my doors at night and I live in a gated community. I say you can't have too much security.

Playing it safe is playing it smart. I've taken many things for granted but recently started to work on a will and trust for our children. No one considers me a worrywart but I learned a lesson as a child. I took my brothers new bike to the store, left it unlocked outside, and it was gone when I came back.

This occurrence has never left my mind. I know some retirees have weapons like guns. I always carry a knife but my wife insists on only carrying her phone. What makes you secure and insecure?

Day 310 - Judgments

I've been too judgmental my entire life and it hasn't gone away in retirement. In fact, I think it's gotten to the point of concern. I'm going to examine my motives and study it from my perspective. I value every aspect of retirement and have a need to thoroughly study all the different things I've read and heard.

My first conclusion is I judge everything on what I think I know and not on what I think others know. There are other things to consider like effort, determination, honesty and age. If you hold the belief that it's never too late to try anything and you're willing and able, open-minded and a positive thinker, you'll be less likely to be judgmental.

I've also concluded that you can oversimplify by not seeing the complexities of the human condition. I have the mindset to try and encourage everyone. It's my solution to making any conversation, activity and participation in life's journey more enjoyable and worthwhile. I don't have a passive attitude, but rather seek a transformation into being more compassionate and less judgmental. Wish me luck!

Day 311 - Set the Pace

I've slowed down in retirement to be able to enjoy each and every day. In the beginning I thought I'd have too much time on my hands and didn't want to appear old or seem like I had no particular interests or activities planned. Now I think I've set the pace and decided what I like to do or not do. Each task has an expectation and happens at a different pace. I continue to remind myself what I haven't completed.

Although most of the excuses are gone during retirement, things still don't seem to get done any sooner unless they're simple. I continue to get my chores done during the week and reserve weekends for other activities.

I've noticed that my priorities get rearranged too often. This is my latest challenge. I also see a bucket list becoming more important and have given thought to at least the next two or three years. I'm wondering if this is the next stage of retirement. The first year seems the longest because you are making adjustments, assessments and not everything is clear in retirement. I hope I never need a pacemaker!

Day 312 - What's the Use?

I may sound like I've found the true meaning of retirement but I'm only reassuring myself with this journal. It's probably my egotism and inferiority complex that has me guessing what to say next that I haven't already said. Years ago, I read a book about living a purpose-driven life and that's my reoccurring theme, alongside with maintaining my health. That keeps me grounded in the day-to-day.

I'm on a constant lookout for ideas, opinions, observations and any useful information to share. I've come this far without rereading anything I wrote and hope to discover more useful tidbits.

Is there a beginning, middle and end of the first year? Sure, but just as I'm a little stuck without ideas today, how I deal with it may lead to a pearl of wisdom. I think I'll continue to make these observations of life the rest of my days. I just heard Bob Dylan sing, "What's the use of wondering why babe, if you don't know by now?"

Day 313 - The Long Haul

Yesterday's uneventfulness has left me and I met someone today who amazed me with the fact that he has been retired for thirty years and enjoyed all my questions.

He is healthy, hasn't run out of money, still has a spouse and is happy with my excitement about retirement. It was only half way through our dinner conversation that he mentioned that I sure had a lot of questions and wanted to know if I was writing a book or something? His wife joined in and asked about our retirement and made us aware of what she believed. She said the world and retirement are going to continue to change but not necessarily for the better.

Wow! I sure wish I had more time with them to learn more about their good will and generosity to leave a legacy behind. I don't foresee that for myself but it can be done in a smaller way. He told me his best advice was to prepare as if it's for the long haul. He added, "You may get sick or hit by a bus tomorrow, so enjoy each day."

One example he shared is that at the age of eighty-five he spent $30,000 on implants rather than get dentures. He said he was glad he did it. I don't think he was as rich as he was smart. He was so amused by my expression he opened up his mouth and smiled! I will never forget the beauty of that face.

Day 314 - Happy Birthday

It happens sooner than we like in retirement and it seems to come sooner each year. It's my 64th birthday and I may not actually feel old, but who's kidding who? I am old and it's not just a number and yes, I'm lucky to be retired. The milestone birthdays of 21, 30, 40, 50, etc., come to a head at the so-called retirement age of 65, 66, or 67, depending on your birthday year. Social security keeps going up and up in age because we supposedly live longer.

In the past, I made a big deal of the birthday celebration by going on an adventure. I think that in the last 35 years, I may have worked on this day only five times. That was only because I chose to. Last year I remember working and saying to myself it would be the last time I would work on my birthday because I'll soon be retired.

Birthday wishes continue to be enjoyed and I particularly reflect on all the different relationships I have and how they have come and gone. During my birthday dinner I received a small dessert with a candle. Do you know what I wished for? I'd like to have another happy birthday.

Day 315 - The Day After

What can I expect the day after my birthday? Would I begin a new year with more clarity, appreciation, gratitude and compassion? I'd like to think it's possible if I make an attempt. I'd like to know what's ahead but none of us do. I've begun to think more about the past and have reached out to old acquaintances including good friends I haven't spoken to or seen for decades.

I've been somewhat lax in maintaining a diet, exercise and a general attitude of well-being. Because I'm beginning my next year, it's an opportunity to set some goals and accomplish more of what's important in retirement. I won't be sad that being 63 is over but rather glad that it happened.

For some reason I think that life will be different in retirement and I'm defining day by day what that means. If you're not enjoying each day of retirement then something's wrong. I'd say remember some days will be better than others and new beginnings can happen any time you want.

Day 316 - I Just Can't Help Myself

We all could use some help and advice in retirement. I think of it as a new permanent situation, yet many folks I've met have gone back to work, mostly part-time. Not me. I've gone over this many times, and I'm staying retired. I'll make concessions and live with less. My wife taught me to never ask less for others but rather ask more of yourself. Good advice!

I can't imagine running out of things to do. I worry more about having to be more willing to ask for help. There are a lot of services for retirees in Florida. I never made use of them in the past and have learned that sometimes your time and abilities will change in retirement. I have seen some retirees over-ask for help and appear needy. I've begun a slow acceptance of letting go of trying to do everything myself.

I also believe retirement is the time to become more honest with yourself. I no longer will climb ladders and go onto my roof. Getting our kayaks on top of the car needs to be reexamined as far as options, my shoulders aren't like they once were. Retirement isn't about total independence and risk-taking. When you can ask for help, you'll be doing yourself a favor.

Day 317 - Over Analyze and Under Utilize

I'm constantly using my body and mind to experience the best retirement I can. Writing this journal every day has made me focus. I don't know what I'm going to say but I'm convinced we should try to reach some greater potential in each endeavor.

I've surprised myself with being interested in giving everything extra effort. In my school years I only occasionally got an A and was a definite B student. I bet if I went to school now, I would strive for the best grade.

I've been self-motivated most of my life but now in retirement I love to get encouragement from my retiree peers. We all can see that effort and results are interconnected. Retirees need each other to help with the obstacles and defining what we can and cannot do.

Many of us have never utilized all of our talents and I've seen many of us exhibit some great potential. We have so many different work experiences, family raising, travel, sports and hobby interests that we should share them with others. I hope someday to utilize more of my personality traits and get an A for effort.

Day 318 - Activities

I call anything I do in retirement an activity. Two or three a day is my maximum. The rest comes along and gets my attention anyway. Today we are faced with going to the ocean and seeing the extent of red tide. It's a nasty browning of water that has killed many fish and kept people away because of the smell and has caused respiratory concerns. We also are going to have a nice lunch and see a special art exhibit.

All the activities were planned in a specific order for a specific purpose. I'm not overly rigid, inflexible or set in my ways. Retirement has me leaning more towards the opposite. I try never to put too much on my plate. I've refilled my plate more than necessary on several occasions but who's counting?

Sometimes I wish I had an activities director. Other times I'd like to see the menu and decide if activities du jour will do. I know that I like variety and especially dessert. What's on the menu for tonight?

Day 319 - Let's Time It

We went kayaking today and spent about four hours on the water. The site was only ten minutes away and set up and take down took another half hour. This amount of time and energy suits us fine. When I had my store, I recall I always set time allotments for work projects and the expectation had to be met. I got paid and made money based on this approach.

I like the freedom and flexibility of retirement but realize my resources and energy level are based on a time allotment as well. The one thing to never do in retirement is to overdo. The consequences are greater than fatigue.

In Florida we drink a lot of water all the time, use sunscreen and remind ourselves to be mindful of the heat. I've also taken the attitude that some things take too much time. I think that about golf and that's why I don't participate. A good friend of mine plays three times a week and brags about not improving one bit. He's not retired and likes to be outside.

I seldom can be convinced to drive very far for dinner unless there's an occasion, pretty view or bargain pricing. You know the early bird special! I don't view this in retirement as time management but rather just being more practical. Both are important in retirement.

Day 320 - Practice and Performance

I've surprised myself with some of the things I do like pickleball, gardening and playing my dulcimer. I actually want to achieve a satisfactory state of accomplishment, at least in my mind. I practice these things with a zest and zeal that hasn't waned. I hope to perform my music, show off my garden and play pickleball in a tournament.

I think of them as achievements that I could present and share with enthusiasm. It's more than just show and tell. I don't mind being judged and revealing the truth about these actions and I hope that my achievements can motivate others. I'm not ready to join a league, enter a master gardening class or become a street musician but I've given each one some consideration.

I now see the benefit of practice and actually think these are my current goals. There are many of us who like to challenge ourselves and have others join us in the fun. I made a bold move to sign up for a music workshop. The experience I have is enough to get me in, but how I will fit in and how well I will do does concern me.

Retirement hobbies don't need to be competitive. I would rather not compare myself to others but it's hard not to. At this stage in life it's about progress because perfection may be out of the question.

Day 321 - Read All About It!

Retirement and reading have given me an opportunity to become more informed and the entertainment value is rewarding. Each week I encounter new things that interest me to learn more.

Today I plan on reading for hours on a variety of subjects and I'll become informed, knowledgeable, entertained and inspired without even trying hard. I'll even have time to watch some YouTube to further my understanding of subjects that interest me.

I've narrowed down my interests during this entire first year of retirement. The process and progress is not without self-doubt, reassurances and value. I'm reading mostly today to actually rest my body and exercise my mind. My wife reads more than I do and usually reads every night before bedtime. I prefer to read in the mornings. Occasionally I've chosen to try a late afternoon read before dinner but I end up napping.

I once envisioned having a complete understanding of a topic but now even with more time available, I'm not sure that retirement is the best time for in-depth study. I have taken on this journal and will someday make my own YouTube video!

Day 322 - Enthusiasm

Retirement has renewed my interests, reestablished my priorities and rejuvenated my enthusiasm. I'm lucky to have found like-minded individuals who have shown me that you should not let age be the main factor in your actions. I was in my mid-thirties when I was introduced to windsurfing and thought I was too old to start learning.

Now, thirty years later with many adventures to share and so much fun, I thank my brother for his encouragement. Many of the feelings I've expressed in this journal are from the mind and heart and I often can't decide which one is more important. Retirement can offer similar experiences.

After a short exposure and some modest experience don't second guess yourself, but rather look for enthusiasts that share this feeling. I won't stray from priority one which is to stay healthy in retirement and I'll continue to use this as a guiding principle. There have been ho-hum days and I have quickly changed my focus without enthusiasm to help me. After you get past this obstacle, you'll need some fortitude to lead the way. It works much better when you work it!

Day 323 - Relax

When it's time to take it easy or relax you've learned a valuable lesson in retirement. If you want to pretend you're on vacation to rest, and are recharging, refreshing and revitalizing your body, mind and spirit, that's ok. Just remember you can't be there forever even if you're retired.

I had an easy-going attitude all day today. I don't regret it but it took me a long time to unwind. Many times during retirement, I've seen it's almost noon and I start feeling like I'm wasting time.

On the weekends I don't usually feel this way. I'll tell myself it's ok, relax buddy, enjoy it while you can, easy does it, cool your jets! We all learn to relax differently and I've found myself sitting in a chair reading or watching TV until some excitement happens and drama unfolds to where I say enough of this.

Other times it's just the thing I need. I've meditated in the morning many times in retirement and like it when I feel renewed and focused. Creating a situation and having a setting is what I find most beneficial.

Day 324 – How Does So Much Fun Bring So Much Good?

Is everything in life work? Can everything in retirement be made more fun? I recognize a cause and effect relationship in retirement. I'm not a big believer in the mind over matter way of thinking. Each day I try to live life on life's terms and not complain too much, lowering some expectations, and making it a good day.

I can't control others, they most certainly affect me, but I have learned to react differently with a simple "think before you speak" attitude. I once had a drinking problem and things didn't need to go badly for me to drink. Once I quit drinking and became more accepting it was easier to cope. I haven't mastered this approach but I'm inclined to tell myself that drinking wouldn't do me any good and I wouldn't enjoy the outcome.

I can honestly say I have never given anyone the finger. I've been given the finger many times and certainly sometimes deservedly. I won't give it back because it's more of the same without resolve or purpose. I'd even say it's childish, like sticking your tongue out.

Why bother to offer the gesture to someone you don't know, understand, like or care about. I know I've been the person driving 30 miles an hour in a 45-mile zone. I also have become more of a person who doesn't care what others think. If it's not fun and doesn't do any good then I'm not interested.

Day 325 - Play Some Music for Others

I belong to a dulcimer music group and today we played some tunes for assisted living retirees. It was a gig and we got invited based on previous exposure. Many of the group's members are in their seventies and eighties and could very well soon be in assisted living based on their age.

We normally just play for ourselves, but we really enjoy playing music for others. Every so often our group leader says it's time to perform for others. It gives us more reason to practice. This is just one thing we can do for others that they will certainly enjoy.

There are many things to consider doing for others. A friend of mine does meals on wheels. Others I know volunteer at community centers, churches and fund-raising institutions. All of these places have a lot of older folks there to help.

I don't volunteer that often but now see that you can enjoy these experiences as much as the recipients. I can still see the faces on the people we entertained and appreciated their thanks. On the way out I wondered where could we go next and play some music for others.

Day 326 - Leaving Town

Why does it take me so long to prepare to leave town? I am more cautious in retirement so often I double-check everything. My wife and I each take care of different things. We both enjoy the anticipation and are planning more trips soon. I can recall six trips this year and each time I had to make arrangements for the newspaper, mail, trash, watering the plants and care for our dog Scrappy. We always pack at the last minute so we don't fuss about which clean clothes to bring.

This next trip is for four days so I'm at ease about not being gone too long. Our next trip which is to Chicago will be eight days and we will spend it with friends and family during Thanksgiving. I know some retirees don't like being away from home that long. If it's a travel vacation many more of us don't mind being away.

I always thought I'd do more traveling in retirement but leaving town concerns me more than I thought it would in regards to familiarity and comfort. I hope old age isn't setting in. Maybe I should go to bed early before our trip.

Day 327 - Road Trip

Up before six and leaving at seven for Universal Studios/Orlando was exciting. My wife and I decided to try an amusement park only two hours away. We haven't been to one in twenty years and we found a midweek deal.

I decided there must be a smart way to see and do all the activities, shows and rides at the park. We walked to the far end and made our way back to the entrance. We saw some shows, had lunch and were reminded thrill rides are not for older folks who are retired, at least not for us.

I'm not kidding, they were rough on both of us. It was fun and daring but I wouldn't recommend it for retirees unless they know what they are getting into. There were both virtual and actual rides. Both come with a motion sickness warning.

My wife told me after a few tumbles, the extreme rides should be avoided and I quickly agreed. We survived about six rides and if you're bold enough to also try, start out with the not so rough and slowly increase the intensity.

Retirement visits to amusement parks may have you thinking about being young again but you may also ask when this aversion to thrill rides began? Are we too old for this? Be careful what you wish for! I did enjoy the people watching and considered it one of the best parts of the trip. I doubt anyone noticed us as the two retired folks going on thrill rides but if they did, good for both of us.

Day 328 - Time Share Deal Anyone?

My wife and I agreed to listen to a time share presentation while we were in Orlando. We spent the first day of our trip in the amusement park and today we got amused at the time share experience. In fact, our hotel stay and amusement park visit were part of the deal in exchange for some discounts.

We were given a sales talk that was about two hours long. Little did I know about those two hours turning into four. The discount they offered got us interested and we didn't know anything about time shares so agreed we had nothing to lose.

If you're retired and are given an offer for a cruise, hotel stay, time share or anything that sounds great make sure you can afford it. The deals are good but the presentations are done by professional sales people who are very good at convincing you that you deserve whatever they're selling.

Better yet, be prepared to have them be willing to explain each detail through multiple experts which they call over to their desk. I won't discount the deals (no pun intended) but if you can afford it and truly think you'll use the offer to its full capacity fine as there are thousands of people who have done just the same though I've heard many complaints.

Other things to ask yourself are, "Do you want to hang around crowds? Do you feel like the cost is worth it? Could you do better with some other loyalty program? You don't have to be a retiree to be a sucker, or informed and even get a second opinion. We felt like we made the right decision and yes bought in.

Hopefully we made a wise decision by getting past the cost concern, knowing if we use it often enough, we will save some money. It's simply a loyalty program for them and sold as a savings program to you. You'll still have to do all the planning, scheduling, research and in our case add the cost to our retirement budget. I think it takes about ten years of use to make it worthwhile.

Day 329 - Fun at the Park

Yesterday's time share deal took more time than anticipated so before heading back to the park we wanted to iron out more details of the time share deal. We spent all day at another amusement park but weren't as adventurous as our first day.

Retirees like me like to learn as we go, but my wife tells me to learn before you go. We thought we'd handle more safe rides and see the sights but we gave up earlier than expected. We went back to the hotel and relaxed at the pool.

We agreed that maybe if we have grandchildren, maybe then we'll come back to an amusement park. There are many different kinds that cater to children and Disney has Epcot are good alternative for retirees.

On the way back to the hotel we also concluded you don't know anything more in retirement than you knew before. We may have forgotten that technology has been introduced to amusement parks as well. Right now, I'm glad there's a pool at the hotel.

Day 330 - New Sights

We headed home after our four-day vacation but had a few stops in mind on the way. We may not pass this way again and there are some interesting options. I'm not in a rush and reminded my wife we are retired and can get home at any time. We visited Mt Dora and Winter Park Florida and we're glad we did. We even said we would come back again.

On the way home we spoke of other places to consider, some near and others far. I think traveling for me is a three-part deal. First there's the planning, then the trip itself. The third part is discussing on the way home what you liked or didn't like and making a commitment to the next trip. I hear Saint Augustine is nice and not too far or expensive.

Day 331 - Changing Your Mind

I woke up in my own bed after our trip to find my wife in a panic about our purchase of a vacation timeshare. She told me she was up until 3:00 am looking at all the papers we signed and read more information on the computer from others who liked and didn't like what they signed up for.

She had some buyer's remorse and she was sorry but we needed to rescind the offer. You can get out of a time share according to Florida law so that's what we did within the time limits.

It wasn't just the cost she was concerned about; in fact, the obligation of having to have to do something changed her mind. I was never totally sold on the timeshare either but I also didn't think it was a bad idea. There was no point in changing her mind so we cancelled our membership and obligations which didn't begin for ten days.

We spent hours deciding to buy and minutes returning the contract. It was a relief I won't forget soon. My conclusion for retirees is to never do anything not 100% thought out and get a second opinion from an unbiased person before you decide. Money and wellbeing are never worth the stress of any commitment.

Day 332 - Opportunities for Service

I haven't taken on any volunteer work and think if a cause comes along that I believe in and see that I could make a difference, I'll volunteer. It sounds like an excuse or at least a delay of action but for now it's the truth.

I've spoken to other retirees and they are about fifty-fifty on doing volunteer work. Some of them do it right away after retiring and others perhaps as selfish as I am, at least for the time being, say they don't want to schedule having to be somewhere each week.

I've asked them what would it take to have them do some volunteer work and most of them said they'd do something if someone else they knew talked them into it. My good deed and service work of the past were always worthwhile, beneficial and a feel-good experience. Even when I did the same work at the same place, the different people involved each time made it a new experience that was revealing to me about myself and the individuals.

My only real objections were working with difficult people who like to make a fuss and think they have the solution. I'm not proud of my self-serving ways and consider it a character defect that I'll address with some prodding.

Volunteering is one of the best ways to overcome isolationism, shyness and fear of the unexpected. It also does so much for the recipients that your actions are much appreciated and often the saving grace of humanity.

I encourage each of us to get out of ourselves, out of the house, and do some good, you'll enjoy the company of others and share in the benefits of making a difference. The good you do will do you good. I've practically convinced myself to find something today that will be an opportunity for service and do some good.

Day 333 - What Are You Busy With?

Have you recently walked into a room and forgot why you were there? I did it twice today and I think it's because I'm easily distracted. The only benefit to this is I'm never bored and can jump from one task to another.

Retirees like to keep busy and have been told it's good for you. Some retirees just look busy or act busy. They have an excited state of mind and act differently in front of different people. I'm not sure if it's a retired person's cover or an adjustment that hasn't yet been made.

I typically stay active and only stop when I'm hungry, tired or it's late in the day. I look ahead to the two or three things I have in mind for the day, but don't mind if I get interrupted. I'm even ok with someone or something disrupting the flow. However, don't question my choice of what's important because I chose it for a reason.

The retirees I've met who are organized and happiest do more and complain less. Just ask my wife! It's her best advice to me. The honey-do list she gives me never goes away and I'm glad someone cares enough to involve me in their life. A live and let live philosophy has come in handy during an unsuccessfully planned day. We're retired and flexibility is now a virtue. I just need to get used to it.

Day 334 - Mix It Up Again

Who would ever give how to spend retirement so much thought, get a plan in place, organize the finances, come to an understanding or agreement with their spouse, and then change everything? I did just that more than once. I consider myself a spokesperson of retirement based on my experience and casual conversations, readings and observations.

I ask a lot of questions to my retired friends and anxiously watch my newly retired wife's actions. I've told many of these folks about my journal and they are happy to share information and opinions. My retirement is simple, flexible and I can't complain. Now why do I want to mix it up, with a new routine and changed schedule?

Not even the first year of retirement gives me insight as to what should come next. I wouldn't call it an experiment but as good as change can be, I think improvement is better. I've learned when I play my dulcimer to mix up the tunes and divide the practice into three parts. First, I loosen up and play random chords and scales. Next, I play a tune list and finally I jam in hopes of creating an original tune.

I didn't invent this idea; it was what I was taught and it works. I play longer and progress more. Once you make up your mind to want more improvement and decide on a path, you need to stay focused. Don't try to reinvent the wheel but rather learn to enjoy how it works.

Day 335 - Don't Ever Be Discouraged

You may decide that what you are doing in retirement is your choice, it makes sense to you and no one should bother caring. You waited a long time for it and you are doing it with an "easy go, easy does it" attitude. If you see that your actions could be different and have some discouraging experiences that's normal and only indicates that things could be better.

You decide and don't ever make concessions without realizing there are other possibilities worth exploring. Where to go next and seeing why you are in this new situation is just part of life.

I'm a big critic and value encouragement to overcome my doubts. As you age and retirement changes knowing what to do next is a big concern. Those retirees who don't care or have given up may be depressed. Illness can be a big factor in our futures.

Retirees need each other to help us see the truth. We can encourage others by setting an example, and kind words go a long way. As youngsters we heard the teachers and parents tell us, "Try and try again." I am grateful for retirement and all that I can do. Now I need to do more for others.

Day 336 - Do it Yourself

It seems like no matter what I like or prefer, I usually think I could or should have done it myself. I am not an expert nor do I have any more experiences than anyone else. I learned from my mom, "You made your bed, now sleep in it," works for staying grounded. I don't do anything electrical and I'm as bad as other older folks with anything having to do with technology. I have an open mind and want to at least try thinks.

Retirement, for many of us, may not be the best time to adopt a do it yourself attitude. It's also not a time for many of us to just think, don't worry about that; let someone else deal with it. How about a compromise?

Information on how to do anything is on the Internet. Books on every subject are plentiful. Family, friends and neighbors aren't too far away for advice. Not having the tools is a hindrance but not having experience isn't always a good excuse.

I'm faced with trimming a large oak tree in my front yard which has branches overhanging the street. I have been instructed to attend to this matter by the community organization that oversees the neighborhood. I have experience, tools, time and will even agree with their assessment. I also see the next-door neighbor had his done by a professional and it looks good. I'm going to do it because I have to and I'll save money by doing it myself. The result is what concerns me and thankfully my wife said she thinks it will look fine.

Day 337 - Bring It On

Retirement can be challenging if you weren't looking forward to it. I had a notion that I could retire sooner than I did but that idea was dispelled with a look at the finances. The cost of healthcare alone changed my mind. Once I overcame each of these obstacles, I got my ducks in a row with a date and direction in mind. After these eleven months of trial and error, changing it up, I've taken on a bring it on attitude!

No fear, no second thoughts, just a simple approach of trying as many things as I like and asking if it serves me or others well? I'm awfully hesitant to make any more insights, express opinions and assume that I have come to terms with retirement. I've been honest about why I am doing what I do.

My courage has come from experience. My know-how has also given me confidence. I want everyone to enjoy retirement and tell me what they like about it. "What's not to like," isn't a good response. Those not so good days aren't looked upon as good or bad but rather an opportunity to live another day.

Day 338 - Time Management

Retirement is really about continuing to make decisions and manage my time. I can choose to sit on my porch or in front of the TV all day. Although so far, I haven't done that. I haven't gotten bored even once. I don't worry too much about tomorrow because I'm honest about getting things done.

When I think about going back to a job the idea gives me the shudders because I'd have to have a schedule. Retirement is freedom with responsibility. Motivation in life isn't different in retirement.

I now see that my experience has made me a better retiree. I may question whether or not doing what you want when you want is the best benefit of retirement. I also see me asking myself and others, "Did what you did or didn't do get more attention?"

My time management began with learning to see how long it took to do things like mow the lawn, wash the car, go grocery shopping and most other chores. Then I decided if I wanted to continue to give these things the time I do.

Timeframes are important for me to ensure a meaningful outcome. I once worked with someone who often said, "Good enough for who it's for." I never liked what that meant. Doing anything in a timely manner is common sense just like appreciating a job well done. If time is money, I sure would like to know where I can borrow some and how I would pay it back.?

Day 339 - When the Time is Right

Anything you do will be better when the time is right. In most cases, retirement happens when you're ready. It was time for me to spend two days trimming my tree and now that it's done I'll probably do some gardening.

In Florida you can grow two seasonal crops. I heard a lot about the farmer's almanac but have relied mostly on observational skills when it involves growing or trimming plants. Most of my reluctances about completing a task were superficial.

While I'm not often lazy I do see some procrastination in my character. I like having a sense of control. If you consider retirement as a right or wrong time, maybe reminding yourself that no one knows the future will lead you to the conclusion that, "Yeah! The time is right!"

Many retirees say things like I'll do it next year or sometime later. I believe the sooner the better, for anything. "When the time is right," sounds like something you say to younger people. Do you think we get younger in retirement? I don't either.

Day 340 - Love Is All You Need

We went to the movie, "A Star Is Born." It's basically a love story with a sad ending. It doesn't deal with retirees, but much younger people, and this reminded me that romance and rekindling your love is something often neglected or forgotten in retirement.

I'm not a romantic because I've never had much confidence. Neither of the main characters ever exhibited much belief in themselves either. The lack of this virtue leads to their tragic downfall.

Most retirees I encounter are married, some more than once and exist as a couple. I wonder about their relationships as a couple and conclude maybe they're together, but I wonder, are they happy? I see my sentiments have grown with aging and retirement, but love is being redefined.

We all have been told you need to love yourself before you can love others. Unconditional love is a concept for me and it's not natural in my life experiences. I never anticipated what being retired with my wife would be like, but seeing each other more than ever before has me rediscovering many things about her.

Loving each other now in retirement may require a new approach or examination of why we came together in the first place, so many years ago. I look forward to someday attending a married couple's retreat and discovering if love is all you need.

Day 341 - Surprise! Surprise!

I've met some amazing people in retirement and you will to if you stay active and look for like-minded individuals. I've met athletes, musicians, artists, writers, business owners, teachers, and many other adventurous types who retired to live the good life that can come after working so many years. If you casually observed them on the street you may never guess anything about them. I'm surprised so often with some encounters with retirees that I look forward to hearing more of their story.

Even a short version of their lives holds my interest long enough to start asking questions. I've also read about many retirees because the local paper likes to feature retirees who choose Florida as their retirement destination. I'd like to make their acquaintance and get more details of the trials and tribulations.

Retirement from one's job leads many of us to surprise ourselves with new activities, goals and opportunities for personal growth, which becomes our new job. All the encouragement in the world may not motivate us as much as seeing others participate in life's choices.

I think I've surprised many of my friends and family members with what I decided to pursue. I'm convinced we make choices as we encounter and overcome obstacles.

If you're willing to share these experiences, others will come along, offer encouragement and help you have a successful, meaningful and fun retirement. You'll be surprised at how much you don't know but it will also open your eyes to so many things that are out there to discover. Participate and enjoy!

Day 342 - What to Avoid

Retirement is the gift that keeps on giving. I thought not having a job, being able to spend my time as I like and trying new things was the most I could expect. I never gave any thought to what to avoid. I've learned now what I like, don't like and most importantly, what makes me happy.

After a few months of adjustments, a lot of questions and giving myself some options, I believe retirement, is as different for each of us as we are different, and should be totally devoid of stress. I can't stress this enough! (pun intended). I am usually calm in traffic jams and have many life experiences to show me how to cope with just about anything.

If on the way to the airport to catch a plane, I encounter a traffic jam that changes everything, my solution for the future would be to try and foresee a potential problem and act according. It's all the unknowns we use as excuses. I like to give myself more time than necessary and go to the airport early, relax and do some people watching.

There's a good reason many retirees go to early bird specials. It's not just to save money and avoid crowds. In Florida, most restaurants are crowded and when you think you're saving money, you may spurge for dessert or have another drink. Retirees learn that there are places they belong and are welcomed.

I avoid people with a big ego and suggest you don't allow them to get the best of you. Communication skills come in handy if you are dealing with difficult people. The best thing to do is remain reasonable, let things work themselves out, and avoid most problems by staying informed and alert. You may not be able to avoid the unavoidable, but you will be able to decide on how to react. Think about it!

Day 343 - Wanting More

Retirement is not the best time to want more. I assume you have assessed your finances, physical and mental condition and want what's best for everyone including yourself. A reality check and some discussions about each aspect are normal things to do.

I needed to be assessed in my pickleball group for a competition and received a two and a half placement. The best players are a five. I am in the middle and while I don't disagree, I want to understand why I want or need more recognition. I do wish I played sooner in life and was more advanced, but will I do what's imperative to gain status? I really enjoy the game and assume with time, experience and coaching, I'll improve.

YouTube is a great place to get help. When I consider everything else I have in retirement like my possessions -- home, car, sailboat, kayak, bike and everything else, I'm grateful and can only hope to continue to be able to enjoy them. I take care of what I have and my health is always on my mind.

I like to think we all believe in never stop improving. Having more or better things isn't going to make a difference if you're not able to use them. I did recently purchase a new dulcimer to improve my musicality. It did make me a better musician because I practiced more and began to sound better. I'm most concerned about being honest with this assessment.

My wife and I have a lot of rock and mineral specimens and only recently decided we don't need or want any more. I have also collected many orchids, but I'm not done learning and would still like more. Wanting whatever you choose in life is normal, but retirement is about choosing wisely. At our age, it isn't about what you leave behind but rather the memories you create. I'm teaching myself to want less and do more.

Day 344 - Hope is Not a Plan

I had a short conversation with a retiree today. She said I hope this and I hope that so often that I wondered if she always speaks this way. She even said, "Well, what can I hope for?" I wasn't trying to be a wise guy but I told her, "Hope is not a plan." She asked what I meant by that. I recalled the number of times she used the word hope in her conversation and said she needed a plan. In fact, I said all retirees need more than a plan and should consider having plans A, B, C and more.

I'm constantly reminded that things just happen and you need to be prepared. Any plans you come up with can be either formal or informal. Serendipity is a fun way to experience life if you can handle it. In my younger years, I enjoyed what it had to offer. In retirement I think you shouldn't depend on it ending up with any positive result.

When I began this journal, I was concerned about knowing if I'd be able to finish it, if anyone would read it and what they would have to say about it? These are all legitimate questions that I hoped to answer. My doubts have not stopped me.

I agree that actions speak louder than words and have given many examples of my plan to be successful in retirement. I've learned that sticking to my plans, a willingness to learn, observing retirees and putting this in writing have not only helped me but I hope that everyone who reads it benefits, and will set their own example. We all can find value in a plan, Do you agree!

Day 345 - What's Next? How Nice of You to Ask!

I met a new retiree who asked me, "What's next for me this fine day?" We played a few hours of pickleball together earlier and this was his parting question. I told him it's Friday and I usually practice playing music, mow the lawn and end my chores early to have a nice dinner either at home or going out.

I added that we had dinner plans with some neighbors who just came back after being away for two months. They weren't snowbirds, just busy with family matters. "Sounds good," was his response so I asked him the same question.

He surprised me with saying he only has one real interest and playing tennis in an over-fifty category dictates much of his life. He trains and travels to pursue his passion. He has played his entire life in a competitive league. I complimented his pickleball abilities with our local group and stated he was the best player I ever experienced.

He was only visiting a friend in our community and was leaving town tomorrow for another match. I felt I'd never see him again but would never forget our encounter. I was very impressed with his dedication and skill as well as his polite nature. I'm more of a jack of different trades and he was more of a master of one. He enjoyed his status in the tennis world and wanted to maintain it as long as possible.

At dinner I told of my encounter and because of the admiration I showed I was asked if I got his autograph? It was then that I wished I was having dinner with someone else.

Day 346 - Body, Mind and Spirit…Your Inner Self!

I'm going to listen more to my inner self. Retirement and aging have made me aware that things are changing faster than ever. My predisposition to not overdo it, be careful and ask if I'm sure about this or that, have made me feel much older all of a sudden.

I'm only 64, I am in good health and when I first retired, I thought this retirement needs to last. My dad passed away at 66 and it's always bothered me. The reality is no one knows the fate of tomorrow. At this juncture in life there are spiritual matters I think I should be giving more consideration.

Am I in touch with this belief? How do I find the serenity and peace we all need? My wife has begun a transformation with her body, mind and spirit. She began a diet to lose weight and be healthier, stopped dying her hair and started attending classes on everything from yoga to color therapy. I haven't followed her lead but am anxious to see the results.

I continue my silent prayer and meditations in the mornings and anticipate changes next year. I'm convinced each of us can have a new life in retirement and would like to leave the ways of the past out of it. I look forward to having a renewed spirit and consider it a second chance at living my life. I've chosen to try to read more, learn new things and have daily reflections. I'll continue to search for more purpose in retirement. I hope my inner self can handle it.

Day 347 - Fall, Friends and Fire

I haven't been on the Internet much lately and decided to get caught up. I spoke with two old friends, one of them hasn't heard from me since I retired nearly a year ago. My old college friend comes to Florida each year for a week and we meet for lunch and spend a few hours afterwards exchanging the last year's events.

When my wife and I first moved to Florida we didn't know anyone and we worked full-time for about five years. We didn't make many friends and now being retired I wonder if we'll make new friends as dear as out older friends. Making friends will take an extra effort and it's not easy.

There are plenty of retirees in Florida and each year there is an influx of snowbirds. I've met some great folks in some of my activities and hope my enthusiastic attitude will help me make new like-minded friends. I'll try not to compare some of these new acquaintances with friends from the past.

We got an invitation for a party next week and the theme is fall, friends and fire. The fire refers to a fire dancer who will be there for entertainment. Each and every social situation is another opportunity for friendships and making new acquaintances. I don't think you can have too many in retirement.

Most of the meaningful and worthwhile experiences I've had were with friends. Retirees can make as many friends as they like but even outgoing individuals like me could use some direction.

Day 348 - Next Time

I wonder how many times I said, "Next time?" In retirement I repeat many of the same actions and activities each week. I continue to make the same mistakes of forgetting something or not going over the details necessary for a satisfactory experience.

It's come to the point in my retirement that saying, "Next time," just won't cut it. I'm not in a hurry and actually move along quite slowly. Achieving the essential aspects of each task, having what I need and being organized is not the problem.

I'm perhaps overly cautious, much less risk-taking, and have come to realize there may be much less chance of a next time. The same goes for any purchase of personal items, necessities for the home and doing things that are worthwhile.

I'd like to commit in retirement to doing things differently. Financial affordability is an important factor in any decision, but it shouldn't be the only one. When I was a young man of 35, my father was ill and told me you shouldn't wait for retirement to do all the things you want to do. He only had one year of retirement before he died at age 66. I was motivated by his message from that point on, but always said I either couldn't afford the time or I didn't have the money. I had many years ahead of me before retirement.

That conversation 30 years ago has me thinking about the next time. I hope when I plan to do things in the future, I start out thinking, "Well last time I…" and don't use, Next time I…" as an excuse.

Day 349 - Not My Problem

Problems haven't gone away in retirement. Sometimes they seem to compound. I usually draw the line or put my foot down on involvement when someone tries to make their problem my problem. I'm a reasonable guy and will help anyone who really needs help. I even expect the same from others.

It's a common occurrence that when we share our lives with family and friends, we get the good and bad. I would advise retirees to cautiously not get too involved in other's lives for one main reason. When you begin enabling someone of something, you'll be part of a problem in which there is no easy escape. Sounds harsh and many people say, "Oh what can I do?"

It's ok in my opinion to not share in all of someone's concerns. Many of us take on responsibilities with an open heart and volunteer our services. We help with the grandkids, look in on the sick and dying, go out of our way to be of service and forget our own needs and those close to us. It's a balance your needs with others' needs.

People do take advantage of one another. Any involvement happens because you allow it to happen. Don't let guilt overrule your thinking either. We should all help each other and consider retirement a great time to be of service. But, set parameters, see how it goes and don't make someone else's problem your own.

Day 350 - Optimism

I feel very content today and am filled with optimism. Retirement has given me a renewed interest in sports, music, travel and continued learning. I continue to hear about many illnesses and deaths and see that the world has many problems, but that's life.

The older I get the more I'm able to concede to a wonderment of the good and bad things in life. My grandmother lived to be 105 and managed herself well until about 99. Her life and retirement lasted very long with little change. My grandfather lived to the age of 87 and constantly related stories of his many survivals during the war and illness throughout his life. He told everyone he outlived three doctors.

I've encountered many attitudes in retirement and like to observe how others deal with adversity and change. Is my retirement half full or half empty? This comes up in my optimistic vs. pessimistic thinking.

During this first year of retirement, I keep drinking from the cup and have refilled it several times. Many times, I prefer the cup isn't full and worry that if it is, I might spill it. I think of retirement as a sipping experience and enjoy savoring the moment. What goes in it next is based on my optimism. Staying positive is easier when the cup is at least half full and I know where more of that comes from. Me!

Day 351 - Ride Captain Ride

I haven't sailed or windsurfed or even been near the water because of red tide, lack of wind or too much wind and other commitments to the degree that I can now say I'm desperate. Rather than be upset about things I can't control I took a bike ride today and while it wasn't my first choice of an activity, I must say I greatly enjoyed the scenery.

My mind wandered and I began thinking about what to say about retirement. Should I look for more material of interest and importance? I saw other older folks I assumed to be retired also riding their bikes and was curious how far they rode. My typical ride is twenty miles which I do in about two hours. I know it's not far or fast because plenty of younger riders pass me by.

The funny thing, as my mind was wandering, I began to pretend that I was on the water and my bike was some sort of boat. I truly felt like a kid whose imagination was turned on after being unused for a long time. I thought my retirement had brought out the kid in me because I started laughing and felt real joy.

How "strange" and "exhilarating" could happen at the same time, was a forgotten feeling. I've heard that retirement does bring out the kid in us and so this must be it. The next thing that happened was I wanted to jump off my bike and go into the water with the intention of splashing about. I even yelled out loud, "Here I come," but stopped short of disaster. I hope tomorrow I get to go to the beach because I need a change of scenery. I'm less likely to get hurt there.

Day 352 - Magical Moments

Are there magical moments in life and I wonder if I will have any in retirement? I guess there have been some strange moments with surprises but I haven't had a magical moment in retirement yet.

I saw a sign today in front of a garden while I was walking the dog and it said, "Welcome to my magical garden." Then later in the day on TV I was invited to the magic kingdom and could do so with a special in-state discount. Finally, while throwing out some magazines in the living room, I looked at the back cover of one of them that encouraged me to spend an enchanted magical weekend at a resort nearby. I immediately thought of the tune, "This Magic Moment," and it must be a sign.

Could I have enticed these magical moments somehow? A sunset, romantic music at a restaurant and some moonlit evenings are some things I've experienced in retirement and they could be considered magical. I may have expected these things to happen but I felt somewhat surprised.

I thought that there are really only two types of magical moments. There are those that you create and those that are just destined to happen. I wasn't even paying attention to these things and they all happened. How do you explain enchantment and romance? Is love like magic? We may not always be able to explain magic or even agree that it exists but I'll bet you I can learn a trick or two in my retirement.

Day 353 - Preservation and Presentation

Retirement has made me overly cautious. I've developed criteria for risk, change and safety. I can't plot out my day or begin any activity without asking questions. Answers to, why, how long, how much and are you sure, will be considered.

When I had a picture framing business, we always stressed preservation before presentation. Our goal was to preserve what we were framing and present it in a conservation setting with aesthetics given secondary status. We wanted it to look nice and it usually did.

Retirement is ending up the same way. I'll take the time to prepare all day for the following day's activity. If I've pushed myself and it's been a strenuous day, I make sure the following day isn't too busy and I can recuperate. Injury is always to be avoided. You can call me a wimp, but I'm having too much fun in retirement and have many things I look forward to.

When it comes to presentation, I'm more aware now of how retirees look and while I need improvement and hope to do so, I don't aspire to ever be considered as dapper. I was never a cool guy either. It could be worth the effort and I could try for a day or weekend to see if I can make it last.

Some retirees always look good and I'm a little envious. As much as my wife fusses over being comfortable, I fuss over not being too good looking. I can still have my fantasies, right?

Day 354 - A Little of This, A Little of That

First thing this morning my wife asked me again, "What's on your agenda?" She, of course, assumes that I have an agenda and I know what I have planned. Not today. I told her nothing really and I thought I'd do a little of this and a little of that. She knows about my routine and how variety is what I strive for but questions my philosophy of engaging the body along with the mind.

Retirement is going along fine but there are still many practical things that need to be done. I told her the spirit part of me guides me when the ego lets go. It's then that I become more flexible and want to be of service to others. I don't remain this way because I have a selfish character defect that I'm working on.

I love to engage other retirees with their retirement plans and day-to-day activities. My curiosity never wanes and I'm seldom disappointed with their responses. Sometimes I think we need others to bounce ideas off of and get insights and encouragement for direction.

I tell myself and others not to just go through the motions, but to do things with a heartfelt desire or need. I've got my share of insecurities, fears, doubts and inexperience to slow me down. My solution is to mix it up with enough variety. Build your confidence with an honest appraisal of yourself or ask others for an evaluation. Egos have no limits.

Retirement has a beginning, middle and end. Taking risks will help make your story more interesting. Try a little of this and that. It may help you find what you were looking for.

Day 355 - Keeping it Real

I went windsurfing today. It is my most favorite thing to do. When I was introduced to the sport at the age of 34, I thought I was too old to learn. After 30 years of windsurfing and encountering different wind conditions, living in Florida with ten months of sailable weather and being retired has allowed me to can enjoy the sport more often. But, I've started to realize I may have to limit my time in the water.

My abilities have changed and I don't like taking as many risks on the water as I used to. It doesn't have to be a thrill sport every time. I can sail on quiet waters and enjoy it at slower speeds. I never was a diehard big wind guy either.

While out sailing today I met a 68-year-old sailor with just as much experience but he could not get enough big thrills with 15-20 knots of wind. He was visiting from out of town and when I said the wind is pretty good this time of year, he responded with he hadn't sailed for a while and needed a wind fix. He also wanted to know how often I was able to windsurf. I joked and said, "Not enough."

He told me he likes to keep it real. His passion for the sport was obvious and I knew that time on the water is exhilarating yet for each of us it was also limited. I immediately thought, I wish I could do and feel like that when I'm his age. I'll have to take some precautions, be well rested and not go out in big winds but to keep it real while fulfilling my passion will mean knowing the risks. Who thought retirement had risks?

Day 356 - Easier Said than Done

My goal since the first day of retirement has been to study the day-to-day experiences of my retirement and share what I've learned with others. I would consider the first year as a stepping stone to getting where I think I'd like to go. Contentment and a fulfilling retirement are on the horizon. After that, I hope that all I've learned will be put into action.

I've reviewed what I have and have not done. I continue to try to follow my own advice. My comments and observations in this book reflect my perspective and my needs and wants. I'm sure to discover more ideas and continue to appreciate the diversity of retirement and retirees.

My wife and I have come to many agreements and look forward to the next year. I already think next year is going to be different. I know more. Some of my deep thinking or insecurities may pass and I'll be more content with knowing I have experience and there's more to get done.

A slower pace seems to be the new norm and above all it's good to be able to have something to look forward to. I'm much better at acting on my intentions. The forces of aging are giving me all the more reason to get things done and enjoy each day.

Day 357 - Do It Right the First Time, It May Be Your Last

I've reached the age of retirement and have had enough experiences with it to say it took a long time to get here so I want it to be fulfilling and last a long time. I have a conflicted sense because so many men I have known have passed in such a short time and only half of them were retired. I heard about another acquaintance passing and I'm saddened because not only was he not very old, he hadn't been retired very long.

Today and from now on I'm going to pledge to consider each outcome of any of my actions and accept that although no one knows how many days they have left, each day is a gift that should not be ignored. I don't think any of these men expected to die at this time in their life. I'm sure each of them would say it came too soon. I won't dwell on this but I'll pass on to others their situations as an example of how we don't know the future and shouldn't take it for granted.

I generally have given out advice from different sources after seeing examples in my life and in others and would like to stress the importance of following a plan to get expected results. I was challenged in my music class today and asked myself, "Is it better to learn to play ten tunes well or to play one hundred tunes poorly?"

The obvious answer wasn't obvious to me because I had to complicate it with some questions. I then decided that in my second year of retirement my goal would be to learn to play fifty songs well. Half of them would be of my own composition and I'll listen to my teacher's advice more often.

I won't be writing about my second year in my retirement, but will use what I have learned this year. I pray getting it right the first time can help me and others succeed, and if not, then maybe we'll get more time to get it right.

Day 358 - Testament

Today my wife and I went to finalize a will, trust and deal with other end of life decisions. It's something each retiree needs to consider doing, and the sooner the better. It's not a simple task and requires a lot of reading but you will be glad when you realize the time and money it will save.

Before I retired, I knew having a will and financial security would help protect my family. But I was guilty of putting it off. I can't imagine anyone disagreeing with the importance. Making the first move is more likely the challenge. I'm glad the decision was finally made and now I can address other issues like healthcare and having a familiarity with assisted living and what it entails.

Without intending to be morbid, everything about your life should now take into consideration your end of life. This new taking action attitude removes stress that retirees do not need. Your last will and testament should also include some parting words to your children. Speak from your heart. You'll sleep better and rest assured when you do the right thing.

Day 359 - Realistic Decisions

I give thought to every detail in retirement and will continue to learn and share my observations long after this first year. I have the will and determination to be honest and consider reevaluation a necessity to fine tune a desirable outcome. A trip to the plant show and sale today put this to the test.

There was a great variety of plants and I went to discover and buy, it's one of my hobbies. This kind of event happens about four to six times a year and I look forward to each one because there's always something new and I generally make a purchase at each one. Some of my plants are placed in the landscape, others that I call specimens are potted and I also replace plants that have died.

I came home today for the first time without making a purchase, yet I spent hours looking at the many new offerings. I even had a coupon in hand, a budget in mind and cleaned up the back of my car to make room for my new acquisitions.

I reflected on two thoughts. Firstly, I don't need any more plants and secondly, I should take better care of the one's I already have. No more plants… well unless one dies and I find some more room to place them. It's easy to make justifications. It's hard to accept realizations.

Day 360 - You Can Over and Under Estimate

I've lived with my retirement routine long enough to say it's fine and works for me. My new observation is I over or under estimate each and every thing that comes to mind. It must be the retirement insecurity syndrome. It can also be considered the learning curve of retirement. You don't know much in the beginning and then as you build up your confidence and extend your boundaries, you find out it's the best thing that could happen at this stage of life.

I hope that those of you who are die-hard job keepers get the chance to experience at least some of what I've experienced, plus more. My newfound freedom comes with a progress report and I'll give myself a B+.

Today is Saturday and I have a full day and night filled with activities. I'm lucky to have a wife who keeps our progress and expectations realistic. She'll often say not to overdo it. I don't go overboard but can become overwhelmed. I was a pretty good estimator in my working career so I put these skills to the test in retirement.

Day 361 - Enlightenment or Acceptance

Retirement is all about acceptance. It's going to be this way no matter what you think. I'm living it and insist on living life on life's terms. If you think you'll go back to work let me warn you, enlightenment may be harder to find. You may be sacrificing serenity, peace of mind, acts of kindness, self-discovery, fulfillment and so on, and for what? You don't have to accept my interpretation. It's my opinion and though I'm not about searching for enlightenment I do see acceptance as an absolute in retirement.

I came to believe this only after arguing about things that didn't matter. So much in the world is harsh, unfair and evil. Today I heard the news about an individual who killed eleven people in a synagogue and I can't get over it without thinking about being harsh, unfair and evil back to them. It won't do any good and I'll never really know why things happen.

We all need to accept that although we may not be able to easily change our society, we should still help those in need. Many of the victims were retired and I could only imagine the pain their families and friends endured. Offer yourself as you see fit and if you become enlightened, remember to share it with others.

Day 362 - Time Management

I'm guilty of being a clock watcher and during retirement letting the time pass is an acceptable occurrence. Most of the things I do have a time structure associated with it. For example, I go to pickleball for two hours on Mondays, and Fridays, mowing the lawn takes 45 minutes, music group meets for two hours on Tuesdays and Thursdays.

Sometimes my expectation and other times my energy capacity affects whether or not I go and how long I stay. I believe in spending my retirement time wisely and while I think it is important to evaluate everything I've done this year, I won't put as much pressure on myself going forward. Next year is approaching and I hope to be more accepting.

I've read, studied and questioned just about as many issues that I could think of. There are more ideas out there and you'll discover them on your own based on your level of desire. To be honest, I haven't reread any of my entries but will get some help with editing after this week.

I'll also add I don't want to write any more about retirement once this journal is completed. I've managed to surprise myself with the ideas covered in this book and believe that each entry could stand on its own. The opinions and observations were presented based on what happened to me.

During this entire process I was time conscious and tried to write about the same amount of information each day. I hope to be less of a clock watcher but it's helped me accomplish my goal. I'm so glad to be retired, can you tell?

Day 363 - Engaged

Retirement has the potential of escaping your complete attention. You may be having so much fun that you don't need to question how's it going without immediately thinking it's great. Writing about it has engaged me for the purpose of learning what to expect and reporting on my personal experiences. I'll share anything and everything retirement related for everyone's benefit.

After nearly a year in retirement, life has gotten easier because I've let go of the past. The working years have slipped from my memory. I will however mention that you should be aware that some new bad habits can easily form. Watching more TV and eating more food are big attractions for me that I need to reckon with.

Don't doubt yourself with the lack of experience in any new activities because many retirees are just like you. It will come if you let it. Volunteering, part-time work, and old pursuing new and old interests are just some of the things that will keep you occupied and fulfilled. After that, staying engaged is the best thing you could do.

The way to stay focused is to be with like-minded individuals and be encouraging. If you don't use what you have, find what you are looking for or you'll end up wondering where did I go wrong?

I started by asking myself many more times than necessary if I wasn't feeling the best about something was it because I wasn't fully engaged? My retirement has shown me the more you give the more you get. It's almost time for me to summarize a few more thoughts, let's leave that for the next two days.

Day 364 - Back to Work?

My original goal in retirement was to not work for one year, decide how I felt and go from there. I've made it with today being one year since I left my last job. I also told myself I would return to my place of employment at the one-year point and see what had changed. I was curious about who was still there, has the place done fine without me and though I was only there for four years, was I missed?

Working at the home improvement store was my transitional job to retirement. I could have stayed there longer and many guys older than me still work there. I was nervous going in and didn't know if I should expect anything besides a handshake and a how are you doing comment.

I walked in later in the evening, the slower time of day, and was surprised to be welcomed by everyone. It made me feel good to know that I was remembered. I got a few hugs and mostly fist bumps. Every time I put my hand out, I got a fist bump followed by a handshake. I wondered when did this new protocol start?

They all told me the paint department has never been the same since I left and I'd be welcomed back immediately. It was nice to hear and my response was after one year of retirement, not working and then experiencing all that retirement offers, coming back and walking into the store was all I needed to do to be able to honestly say, "No thanks, I prefer being retired."

Life was good at work but living in retirement is better. We exchanged our recent experiences and I made sure to speak with enthusiasm when I spoke of what I was doing in retirement. They all soon excused themselves saying they had to get back to work. I thanked them and said, "I know."

Day 365 - Milestone

Being retired now officially for one year is not my greatest accomplishment. I've been fortunate to have had the experience, write a lot of things about it and I look forward to continuing to have a happy retirement. Staying happy, healthy and helpful in this first year of retirement has been a blessing and I'll consider it a milestone from here on.

The thoughts I recorded are not without misgivings or regrets. I've done a lot, seen a lot and know much more than I did when I started. I can't redo anything but I can review any time I want and make corrections for the future. I've come to appreciate that retirees aren't afraid to express themselves and offer much wisdom.

Each milestone, such as birthdays or weddings come at our age with elevated joy. We made it and many don't. I'll soon turn 65, the age in which I think of as old and retirement is due. I look forward to someday soon becoming a grandfather.

Travel is planned and I'm turning into a real musician. Publishing this journal to help others with a glimpse of my experiences, comments on how I would do things and the opinions, often off the cuff, were all meant to inform and entertain. It's a time of celebration again!

In Conclusion

I set out to journal my first year in retirement and can now say I did it. I enjoyed the working years and will certainly enjoy retirement. I realized early about the importance of staying healthy and consider it to be a big part of my retirement. I also will continue to experience money needs, and I encourage each of you, to triple-check your financials, and be prepared to spend more than you think.

Other very important lessons to pass along are be honest with yourself and don't waste time. Remind yourself that the purpose of retirement is to have a retirement with purpose. We all deserve a retirement without stress.

When you retire, where you retire and with whom you retire are some important decisions to make. I'll say for me, the sooner you decide, the better retirement will be, and I think this is true for all retirees. If you go back to work part-time, work as a volunteer or even venture into a new career, count yourself lucky. You have the freedom of choice and the ability to further pursue some new interests.

Throughout this book, I've explored the process of retirement, and the simple truth is, being proactive in retirement is my advice for achieving happiness and making the most of your life. Don't isolate or spend all your time with retirees. Being around all age groups is a way of experiencing the cycle of life. We all can share something. Good times and bad times come and go.

Remember, retirement isn't all about what you leave behind, but rather the memories you create.

Welcome to the retirement club. You deserve it! Congratulations Good Luck!